Telepolitics: The Politics of Neuronic Man

Television has created a new kind of man with a new kind of politics --Telepolitics-- and it has changed democracy as we have known it in North America.

So argue the authors of this brilliant book that could well serve as a handbook for those who wish to take and keep power in America today. Starting off from McLuhan's theories on how technology changes man, they show that it is the form --and *not* the content-- of television that has produced the new age of Neuronic Man.

Neuronic Man --a creature "to be both pitied and feared"-- murders publicly. He is violent, intolerant, and impatient; he wants all his problems solved right now. He rejects the rule of the majority and consensus, by which U.S. democracy has survived for 200 years, and he is forcing ever-increasing fragmentization upon American society. He responds to all stimuli through his total nervous system. He has made politics a matter of personalities --not issues; not the best man, but the man with the best TV image, wins. Those so elected cannot govern by traditional democratic means, but must depend on secret governments --on advisors, super-groups, think tanks, as the society tends not toward the totalitarianism feared by the Orwells, but toward anarchy.

The authors spare no one --neither the great TV networks, nor the major political parties; neither the Pentagon nor the occupants --and would-be occupants-- of the White House of the past two decades. They attack both the New Leftists and the new rightists, the old liberals and the old conservatives, the drop-out kids and those who train and arm secretly, waiting for the day of revolt. All have been equally, and wilfully, blind and deaf to the new reality.

Is there any hope? Can civilization be saved? If yes, then it can be done only by men who recognize that a new order has come upon them unlike anything hitherto known in history --and who search for a new ethic of survival.

Telepolitics was written to stimulate men to do just that. It is a seminal book. Full of insights that illumine the gap between what is pretended and what is, it offers no new answers. But it does ask the new questions.

Telepolitics: The Politics of Neuronic Man

Television has created a new kind of man with a new kind
of politics --Telepolitics-- and it has changed democracy as
we have known it in North America.

So argue the authors of this brilliant book that could well
serve as a handbook for those who wish to take and keep
power in America today. Starting off from McLuhan's
theories on how technology changes man, they show that
it is the form --and *not* the content-- of television that
has produced the new age of Neuronic Man.

Neuronic Man --a creature "to be both pitied and feared"--
murders publicly. He is violent, intolerant, and impatient;
he wants all his problems solved right now. He rejects the
rule of the majority and consensus, by which U.S. democracy
has survived for 200 years, and he is forcing ever-increasing
fragmentization upon American society. He responds to all
stimuli through his total nervous system. He has made
politics a matter of personalities --not issues; not the best
man, but the man with the best TV image, wins. Those
so elected cannot govern by traditional democratic means,
but must depend on secret governments --on advisors,
super-groups, think tanks, as the society tends not toward
the totalitarianism feared by the Orwells, but toward anarchy.

The authors spare no one --neither the great TV networks,
nor the major political parties; neither the Pentagon nor
the occupants --and would-be occupants-- of the White House
of the past two decades. They attack both the New Leftists
and the new rightists, the old liberals and the old conservatives,
the drop-out kids and those who train and arm secretly,
waiting for the day of revolt. All have been equally, and
wilfully, blind and deaf to the new reality.

Is there any hope? Can civilization be saved? If yes, then
it can be done only by men who recognize that a new
order has come upon them unlike anything hitherto known·
in history --and who search for a new ethic of survival.

Telepolitics was written to stimulate men to do just that.
It is a seminal book. Full of insights that illumine the gap
between what is pretended and what is, it offers no new
answers. But it does ask the new questions.

Frederick D. Wilhelmsen and Jane Bret

Dr. Frederick D. Wilhelmsen and Mrs. Jane Bret are among
the new Catholic intellectuals who have been making such
an impact on American thinking in recent years. In
Telepolitics, they combine their diverse experience and
talents to illuminate the effects of television on America.
It is a formidable combination. Their last book, *The War
in Man: Media and Machines,* was chosen the best book
in its field of communications by San Francisco State
College and received its Broadcast Preceptor Award in 1971.

Dr. Wilhelmsen uses his extensive classical scholarship to
keep the book in historical perspective. For the past seven
years he has been professor of philosophy and politics at
the University of Dallas. He holds degrees from the
Universities of San Francisco, Notre Dame and Madrid. He
is particularly knowledgeable about the Spanish-speaking
world, having taught five years at the University of Navarre
in Spain, and for shorter periods in Mexico, Peru and
Argentina. His writings include six books in English, two in
Spanish, and two written co-operatively with Mrs. Bret.

Jane Bret reflects in many ways the new American woman
who, after years spent in home-making and child-rearing,
suddenly emerges as a mature social critic. Born in Louisiana,
she studied at St. Louis and Dallas Universities. She founded
and taught in several Montessori schools, and it was while
working with emotionally-disturbed children that her interest
in communications began. As the wife of William Bret, the
Texas attorney and management consultant to whom the
book is dedicated, she has also traveled widely. The Brets
have four children, ranging from ages thirteen to twenty-one.

Both authors know Canada well. Dr. Wilhelmsen has been
a guest lecturer at Canadian universities, and Mrs. Bret has
appeared on Canadian media during her frequent visits. Their
comments on Canada --also a telepolitical country-- and on
Quebec in particular sharpen by comparison and contrast
their observations of the American scene.

Telepolitics

The Politics of Neuronic Man
by Frederick D. Wilhelmsen and Jane Bret

 Tundra Books, 1972

© 1972, Frederick D. Wilhelmsen and Jane Bret

Published simultaneously in the United States of America by
Tundra Books of Northern New York, Plattsburgh, N.Y. 12901
and in Canada by
Tundra Books of Montreal, Montreal 125, Quebec

Library of Congress Card No. 73-187493
ISBN 0-912766-04-2

First edition: October 1972

Printed in the United States of America

To Bill Bret
whose encouragement and counsel made it possible

Books co-authored by Frederick D. Wilhelmsen and Jane Bret

The War in Man: Media and Machines (*received Broadcast
Preceptor Award, 1971*)
Seeds of Anarchy: A Study of Campus Revolution

Books by Dr. Wilhelmsen

Hilaire Belloc: No Alienated Man
Man's Knowledge of Reality
Omega: Last of the Barques (*personal adventure in four-masted
sailing ship off coast of Peru*)
The Metaphysics of Love
The Paradoxical Structure of Existence

In Spanish

El Problema del Occidente y los Cristianos
El Problema de la Trascendencia en la Metafisica Actual

We enter a new dark ages and what we have known and often cherished will not even be a memory for our children. In order that we might survive in this desolation of withered hopes, we will have to learn to ask the right questions; but we cannot ask these questions unless we first understand what has happened to us.

Table of Contents

Introduction

Section I   The Neuronic

Part I   Neuronic Man

Part II The Neuronic Age

Part IV   Secret Governments

Conclusion

Bibliography

Index

Introduction

The reader of a book which claims to explore the relations between politics and television has a right to know where the authors stand.

The authors stand nowhere. Today there is no place to stand, only to understand.

This answer to a hypothetical reader does not conceal the obvious, even banal, truth that every book is written out of some background, drawn out from some history, evaluated in terms of some set of standards, even if they be anti-standards.

Like Alice in Wonderland we attempt to explore a new world. Our new world is fashioned in the image of electronics. We explore the politics of that world and we seek its logic --or non-logic, or supra-logic. Alice brought to the Looking Glass both the biases and convictions that she carried from the real world. As we roam through the "reel world," we confess that we carry a baggage of convictions and prejudices inherited from the older civilization in which we were born.

Along with other probers in the basement of the new age of mass electronic communications, we go about our business with the only tools we possess. These tools were fashioned within a civilization founded on print, nurtured in the work

13

ethic, and formed within the rhythms of an older mechanical technology.

We have written a book: literacy -- the older technological bias -- has been our tool. We have worked to bring forth this, our labor: puritan seriousness about the intrinsic goodness of hard work has been a spur making possible our document. Our study will be read only by men who reflect about life, who consider the unexamined life not worth living; by men who are not totally cradled in the new world of simultaneous, electronic participation. Our audience will be formed by people who know what distance is; who cherish solitude; who can meditate about ideas in privacy. We presuppose a civilized audience that is interested in the new barbarism.

We do not state in these pages that civilization is better than barbarism. Nor do we state the contrary. Ortega y Gasset once wrote that the only non-civilized values were barbarian values. Possibly barbarism is a superior form of human existence. Possibly civilization has failed. It is even possible that not bookmen but children watching Punch and Judy shows are better judges of the new world in which we live. Puppet watchers may be the prophets for tomorrow. An eye for illusion may be the best map of reality.

We leave the answer to the reader.

Our intention has been to explore the new electronic politics, the politics of Neuronic Man. We have probed and pushed and have tried to bring to light a new social structure, a new world of telepolitical imagery. This imagery is fashioning into history a new man. He is not the old civilized citizen of the national state. He is not even the old tribal clansman, the state's historic enemy in modern times, although he is closer to the latter than to the former. We confess an absolute ignorance as to whether Neuronic Man is better or worse than either.

14

Politics today is a new reality. Man enters into a hitherto unknown order of being because he has been profoundly altered
from within by a new technology. The Age Electric has no
antecedents. The electronic revolution has canceled progress
as a significant dimension of the human spirit. Electronics
has annulled evolution. Speed-up destroys time and growth.
Everything just happens.

Telepolitics touches upon the effects of the electronic revolution in continents and nations that only today begin to enter
the new age, without having passed through paleolithic mechanization. These "backward" nations may well be the wave
of the future because they have no immediate mechanical
past. In any event they will soon be englobed totally within
the new technology. Our concern with these nations and
continents, however, is only instrumental to this book. We
have used them to heighten the lineaments of the environment
of complete electronic information and image-exchange which
is found fully developed only in the highly technologized
North American continent. *Telepolitics* is largely about North
America today.

"To most men," wrote Coleridge, "experience is like the
stern lights of a ship, which illumine only the track it has
passed." This "rearview mirror," as media master Marshall
McLuhan calls it, has prevented the Western world from
seeing the road ahead.

Western technical genius has always prevented Western man
from seeing the effects of his own scientific innovations until
they are behind him. Creativity is blind --like love. Were
creativity not blind, men would have done what they were
going to do before they did it. The West always does things
and then scratches its head as it confronts the corrosive effects
of its own genius. The East scratches its head and then does
nothing at all. This book restricts its observations to the
early doers and late scratchers. In fact, this very book is an
instance of head-scratching after the fact.

15

Predictions about the future are necessarily statements about the past. Futurists are the most finely chiseled of our reactionaries. Therefore we have avoided the temptation of speaking about new revolutions which are just around the corner. The revolution just around the corner seems always to have happened yesterday, just around the corner you just turned.

We see *Telepolitics* as an exercise in political detection. An early reader of this manuscript suggested it be titled *The Prince: Revisited,* insisting that what we have really written is a textbook of power, a how-to-do-it book for the politician on the make.

The exercise of Machiavellian power is cynical because it is self-conscious. The exercise of electronic power, in contrast, has been largely absent-minded. Our media men are cavemen with newly fashioned axes. Alley Oop is neither moral nor immoral. Huntly and Brinkley and Reasoner and Smith and Sevareid are not the children of Machiavelli. These media actors are innocent children, electroded Alley Oops.

If the pages in this book sound frequently as cynical as Machiavelli, this is not because we advocate cynicism. We advocate awareness without which both cynicism and non-cynicism are impossible. The responsible use of power demands insight into the tools and instruments and media of power. In this sense only have we written a handbook.

As a footnote to this, we would like to add the following gloss to Lord Acton's famous statement about power tending to corrupt: "All *ignorance* about power tends to corrupt and absolute ignorance about power tends to corrupt absolutely."

Education, most particularly university education, is massively ignorant about what is happening today. The conspiracy against permitting students to understand their own environment is total. Such principled ignorance about the nature of new electronic *forms of power* is at least as vicious as is any clinical and cynical use of power by the prince. The fastidious refusal to look at the "reel world" of today is the stock in trade of humanist educators and of the official custodians of the liberal arts tradition. Their sin is compounded with the sin of moralistic and puritanical Christians: *they* will not look at the late twentieth century simply because they don't like it! Both are joined by the blank grin of conventional liberalism that thinks all is going well at the very moment when its own cherished world agonizes on its deathbed.

Mounier* once said that Americans made revolutions and Frenchmen talked about them. Americans, historically, have speculated very little about their own role in history. We have not had the time to turn the head of the world upside down because we have been so busy turning its body upside down. To us North Americans of the United States, Karl Marx looks as dusty and Victorian as the London museum he worked in more than a century ago. The United States is as bored by Communism as it is dismayed by corporate capitalism. Possibly --this is a hope-- we may muddle through the coming time as we did through the nineteenth and early twentieth centuries.

Our economy and the very psyche of our youth have been transformed. But the custodians of order have their attention someplace else. They seem unaware even of the new forms of war which are part of electronic politics.

Americans make images daily but we cannot deal with them rationally because of our past. A nation so moralistic as to produce both Cotton Mather and Hugh Hefner cannot understand forms but only anticipated goals. A basically puritan people with a long history of bias against theater cannot take kindly to the truth that electronic politics today has become a show. A fundamentally work-oriented people that always put a premium on high seriousness cannot absorb gracefully the metamorphosis of politician into actor and of statesman into star: e.g. Mr. Nixon in Peking. Americans

*Emmanuel Mounier in *Révolution personnaliste et communautaire*

17

cannot accept that politics in Peking was identically one
with theater, magnificent theater at that. Americans cannot
even accept these facts *as theory*, even though they live them
and are transformed by them as existence.

Even when perceptive Americans do come to grasp the fundamentally artistic nature of the new politics --McGinniss in
The Selling of the President, for example-- they end their
discoveries by asking how we might undo this aberration.
Telepolitics, for them, remains just an abomination.

This profoundly historical puritanism about the supposed
seriousness of politics helps us to understand why otherwise-
sensitive critics cannot probe electronic and political theater.
Even those who are in the theatrical action insist they are not.
They are "telling it as it is." All of us, of course, buy the lie.

Nobody in non-Shakespearean America wants to admit that
politics today is principally a play, a performance.

This moral reaction --"We *are* telling it as it is, damn it! "--
is the aesthetic and technical problem facing every media
consultant of an aspiring candidate for national or state office.
Media consultants are not cynical Machiavellians who lie
publicly when asked by print-journalists what they are up to.
These men really do not believe that they are the wizards
they are. To listen to them talk about their trade one would
think that they are "bringing out" a candidate's own personality rather than fashioning him into a new reality, the reality
of the image. The nineteenth century hangup in the apostles
of the twenty-first century is part of the immoral innocence
which hangs like a cloud over the nation. Politics today is
simply liturgical theater exercised by men who are at home
in neither theater nor liturgy. Don't do as I say: do as I do!

Electronics is not only an extension of man. This is true of
all technologies. Today man is an extension of electronics.
Alley Oop's axe, in its internal mode of operation, does not
reiterate what goes on in Alley Oop's brain. The axe simply

executes its owner's will. But electronic technology in its televised perfection reiterates and parodies processes going on in the human brain. Man, the *creator* of electronics, has become the *creature* of electronics. This man is Neuronic Man-- the subject of our book.

A nation born in a print shop and nurtured by books -- a nation that could have gotten up a sweat about poor George III -- is ill-fitted to contemplate steadily, even with a kind of fascinated horror, the truth that a population once formed of a homogeneous and literate citizenry is dissolving into a vortex of neuronic tribes for whom older loyalties, when known, are hateful. Usually these loyalties are utterly unknown because they are foreign to the dark charismas which are the heartbeats of the new electronic peoples. The latter-day Vikings and Goths have landed on the shores of the consciousness and they swarm over the ruins of what was once modern civilization.

Can democracy survive?

To this and other questions raised by the new technology we address ourselves in these pages. We ask the reader to meditate upon our overriding conclusion: a society created by Telepolitics cannot be governed telepolitically. Not totalitarianism but anarchy is the asymptote of electronic man.

Not the destruction of the past but its almost intolerable return as electronic symbol and dream in an age in which "Time present and time past are both perhaps present in time future, and time future contained in time past" is the electronic eternity of our passing moment in time.

Jane Bret
Frederick D. Wilhelmsen

Dallas, Texas   July 1972

19

Section I
The Neuronic

Part I
Neuronic Man

1 Enter Neuronic Man

A new man has entered history. By all older standards he
is a being to be both pitied and feared. Formed in the image
of an electronic world that mimics the workings of his own
brain, he has become his own TV set. Beamed on from every
angle, New Man no longer exists outside the limits of his own
technology.

Like the couple in Walker Percy's *Love in the Ruins* who
cannot perform sexually except in front of a team of
Masters and Johnson-type scientists who measure their copu-
lating electronically, the New Man knows --dumbly but
infallibly-- that if it isn't tuned on, it simply isn't at all.
Even more: if he is tuned off, *he* has ceased to exist.

New Man murders publicly. Jack Ruby and Sirhan Sirhan do
their thing under kleig lights. Lee Harvey Oswald sees to it
that his debate about Cuba is taped and the records subsequently become collectors' items. Father Manson sends his
children out to kill Sharon Tate in the name of Satan. The
murder is a public gesture, a symbol. After all the husband
of the murdered woman had already celebrated the rites of
Satanism publicly in his *Rosemary's Baby*. The succubus
baby, born as image on the screen, cradled into magical
being, is the creature of a man whose unborn baby is then

daggered to death in the name of his own electronic creature. Image outdoes reality and reality becomes image.

Jet planes are hijacked to Cuba, and to no place as well, by lonely TV watchers who gain one moment of electronic immortality in a gesture that truly makes them *be* for the first time in their otherwise drab and undistinguished lives.

Ideology is irrelevant. An Arthur Bremer stalks, gun in pocket, grin on face, the President and presidential candidates alike, waiting for his moment to enter the electronic stage.

Private becomes public and background foreground. A kidnapped British diplomat in Montreal watches in captivity a television screen that flashes to him the terms of his own release --or death.

Puppeteers become their own puppets. Mask is reality in a Mardi Gras world in which costumed figures swirl from ball to ball in a kind of high camp that marks a very new style indeed of human existence.

The old are shocked by all the bloodletting in current films. But they are shocked because they can anticipate what will happen and they remember later what did happen. Therefore they die three times over. The young cannot anticipate and therefore present violence slides into a forgotten past because it never was a future.

The New Man participates in every war from Biafra to Vietnam and from East Pakistan to Northern Ireland. Therefore he feels no need to move from his chair and get up and fight. He has already fought the war! Vicarious violence weds pacifism.

Both breed impatience. Everything must be done right now. Cosmic petulance agitates the globe.

Purposeless destruction of property serves the higher purpose of anarchy. Where men once walked with pride
pointing to what they had built, the young walk with
arrogance past what they have destroyed.

Masking itself as revolution, this total impatience is in fact
merely the consequence of the only significant revolution
of our time: the technological. As Jacques Ellul puts it:
"--to my great sorrow, I see *all* modern revolutionary
movements making their final agonized lunge at the television screens." *

2 The New Tribalism

It is estimated that the average American will spend ten full
years of his adult life watching television.

Television has created a kind of intense political identification
which, far from uniting men in human sympathy and tolerance, disperses and shatters into mutually hostile groups an
erstwhile monolithic citizenry.

This new decentralizing dynamism is formal. It cuts across
political and ideological divisions even as it renders them more
glaring and abrasive: Black Power; Young Lords; Chicanos
and other Brown Power groups; WASPS; blue-collar workers;
Czech, Polish and Italian Catholics from lower middle-class
suburbs of industrial towns; John Birchers and the United
Jewish Defence League; the followers of George Meany and
of George Wallace; SDS and YAF.

Each of these splintered groups identifies with its like
electronically. The drive is profoundly conservative in that
this identification does not aim at change but at survival.
Haunted by the conviction that some kind of apocalypse is
at hand, each grasps desperately to its own on its own terms.

Autopsy of Revolution quoted by Richard Sobickel in "Marx
is Dead," *Harpers,* April 1972, p.101

Marshall McLuhan vividly demonstrated in *Understanding Media* that the social and personal consequences of any medium --which is always a human extension-- result from the new scale that is introduced into human life by technology. The medium is the message.

The new decentralizing phenomenon sweeping the global village and emerging as cohesive depth patterns of totally-involved kinship groups has been called "tribalization."

But the social critic must move cautiously in denominating the new phenomenon "tribalization" without any further qualifications. The classical tribe as a sociological unit is closely-knit spatially. This is true even of nomadic tribes such as the Great Plains Indians. They carry their space with them: tents, tepees, wagons, etc. These tribes are united against that which lies beyond the spatial boundary of the tribe. Outside the tribe is the unknown.

The tribal origins of the Roman experience are revealed in the word *limes, limites* which originally meant trench. Such trenches suggested the hostile unknown beyond. The classical tribe is hardly distinguishable from a "clan."

Both terms point to a blood relationship which is symbolized in the clan name carried by the clansman. He is first and foremost a McDonald, or a Stuart or an O'Brien. As the clan grows, the initial blood relationship is thinned out biologically but its cohesive and psychical spine remains the common name. The clan, therefore, is almost always governed as though it were a family. And our Western institution of kingship grew out of Germanic tribal organizations described as far back as Tacitus.

The classical "clan" or "tribe" cannot disperse its members without ceasing to be itself, if not in one generation, then in two or three. The one exception to this rule seems to be the Gypsies, some of whose tribes --such as the Kalderash-- have maintained their laws, ritual, language and tribal allegiance, in spite of global dispersal. This possibly makes the Gypsies admirable candidates for the new electronic world.

The new electronic man has lost any sense of space as being a fixed center, whether it be immobile as is the trunk of a tree or mobile as is a wheel. Spatial limitation has been transcended through the new electronic image.

Tribesmen today no longer need spatial contiguity in order to participate in the rites of corporate communion. Therefore we are witnessing the curious phenomena of the revival of *old* tribal loyalties that had almost been extinguished due to the scattering of these groups under the pressures of industrialization and mechanization.

But are the new kinship groups "tribes" in the old classical sense of the term? Their differences would seem to be as profound as their likenesses. The youth phenomenon, a shaggy, bearded army, crawls the world. They dress alike, sport the same hair styles, speech patterns, and cradle themselves in the rhythm of the same rock; they share the same general vision of good and evil. They are all anti-Establishment whatever that "establishment" might be. None of this depends upon any spatial contiguity. Identification has been made, cutting across space *and* time through the electronic image.

This electronic identification is accomplished through television which has become an extension of man's central nervous system. The identification takes place through a participation of all the human senses in a unified way. The new tribesman identifies electronically in the neurons of his brain.

This is why we have chosen to call this new human "Neuronic Man."

What does the neuron do? In man's central nervous system the neuron stores and transmits messages. Sensory impressions are registered at the nerve endings and translated into impulses which run along the nerve cells, arrive at the appropriate centers of the brain and are perceived as sight, sound, pleasure or pain. The neurons also transmit man's sensory messages to the environment outside.

Neuronic Man receives, stores and transmits his messages into and from the moving electrons which constitute the television image.

The image formed on the television screen is a crude parody, produced electronically through art, of what goes on in the brain of a man when he decodes information and synthesizes into unity a sensorial field.

Every man at all times, places, and circumstances is neuronic, but the term "Neuronic Man" is peculiarly appropriate for contemporary electronic man. For his technology not only extends his senses (all technologies extend the senses), but electronic technology extends *all his senses by imitating them in the way in which they act.*

Electronic art imitates the nature of the human brain. This flipflop means that contemporary man literally lives outside of himself in the way in which he lives inside himself. Even more, inside and outside blur and commence to lose their distinction.

Cosmic consciousness is the electronic absorption of the cosmos within a technology that is both the ape and the mirror of man's psychic life.

One might argue that in certain historical situations the nervous system was at the service of the digestive, respiratory, or even genito-urinary systems. The nervous system synthesized the work of all these other systems.

Today, however, the nervous system synthesizes all these other systems for the sake of itself. And whereas the product of the centralized nervous system is the unified image, the product of the electronic revolution is the electronic image. Image has become reality.

We are in the age of Neuronic Man.

The apex of man as the maker of images is the spoken word. The apex of the image-making power of electronic technology is the spoken word. This symbiosis both looks back to the oral culture of the old tribes even as it points to the difference between tribal and Neuronic Man. Participation in the clan is through a real or mythic blood link with the dynastic leader. No mythical blood link causes the participation of Neuronic Man with his televised leader.

The neuronic identification of America and the world with the Kennedy dynasty was wrought in the catalyst of the image. Images sent and decoded on the television screen were then received and decoded within the brain of Neuronic Man. In so doing, wealth, blood, social status, national origin, religion, and ideology were bypassed. The identification was complete. Neuronic Man does not need his participation to be mediated through any conceptual or doctrinal framework. This links him with the older tribal man even as it sunders him definitely away from the print culture of the last several centuries.

Man is a symbol-making animal and all symbolism is a tissue of imagery, of perceptions. No historical epoch was more self-consciously symbolic than was the medieval. Full of heraldry and color, of gestures stiff and stylized, Medieval Man decoded his imagery into symbols according to pre-established meaning or significance.

Neuronic Man today projects his own meaning into prefabricated images. But he follows the image of the significance and not the significance of the image. The more blurred

the image, the more effective is its power. Richard Nixon
can be all things to all men. So can Pierre Elliott Trudeau
in Canada --or *could,* when he first ran for prime minister.
(As his image has grown sharper in recent years, his range
of appeal has grown narrower.)

The diffused tactile sensuality of blue jeans and floppy
sweaters differentiates today's youth from today's middle-aged
generations. The middle-aged still identify sensually only
through the mechanical translation of sensory images into
sharp visuality. Nineteenth and early twentieth century man
translates tactility into visuality: until he can *see* --at least
imaginatively-- what he touches, his encounter is simply a
problem to be resolved.

Neuronic Man translates visuality into diffused tactility.
Playboy's retreat to the Varga Girl of the fifties is an instance
of planned obsolescence, a strategic backward march by the
house organ of old-fashioned mechanical visual man.
The diffusion of sensuality through the electronic image
renders Neuronic Man peculiarly immune to both the gran-
deur and the awesomeness of Newtonian or absolute space.
An executive who is in Chicago one day and San Francisco
the next simply cannot project imaginatively, in any visual
sense, the space he has traversed on jet airplane. The
technicians and scientists in Houston would collapse psychologically if they attempted to visualize what they are up to
when they put astronauts on the moon. Neuronic Man puts
space in the backpocket of his wraparound technology.
He conquers computations, not spaces.

Neuronic Man is foreign to his Renaissance past. The
Renaissance adventurer looked out on an infinite space to be
conquered. This beckoned every buccaneer in continental
Europe to sail beyond the old cut-off point of no return,
the Strait of Gibraltar.

Neuronic Man is hostile to speed, appearances to the contrary. His speeded-up world has abolished speed as a human

experience. Radar is too fast for the speed demon on the
highway. The police siren simply executes the electronic
command. A ticket is the punishment for going too fast.
Speed today is a calculation, as is space. Neither are experienced realities done or executed by men. Time-lag takes
the place of crossing the ocean in a jet. And once you have
crossed the ocean a few times even time-lag disappears.
Neuronic Man is hostile to experiencing what older societies
called "reality." Neuronic experience is the image.

Spaces as well as times exist today as sport. They are tolerated as play. Neuronic Man does everything his immediate
predecessors did: he runs the half-mile; he participates in
the Indianapolis 500; he sails; he hikes; he hunts. He even
jogs for the sake of his heart. But he does all these things
as symbolic gestures which have become a kind of content
within an electronic world that has rendered nature obsolete
and nonserious, playful at best, medicinal at worst.

Shakespearean Man spanned two worlds. Coming out of the
older medieval order, Shakespearean Man sensed himself as
belonging to a hierarchy, as subordinate to a divinely established plan, as occupying a place and playing a fixed role
in life. But Shakespearean Man had discovered something
new: personality in the sense of individuality. This new
psychological emphasis on the "I" went hand in hand with
the discovery of perspective in painting. With every shape
and figure in perspective, painting appears exactly as it does
to the eyes of the individual observer. Space extends
outwards toward an infinity, inviting exploration and conquest by the observer. Shakespearean Man, therefore, was
a tension between an older man for whom the individual
"I" was subordinate to hierarchy and a new man for whom
reality itself existed as it flooded the vision of the individual.
Elizabeth I of England and Francis Drake were splendid
instances of this tension. Drake did his own will all the
while he pretended to be doing the Queen's. As a Christian
sovereign, the Queen publicly repudiated Drake but privately,

as a very liberated female personality indeed, urged him on in his piratical romp through the Spanish New World.

Neuronic Man does not believe in the fixed and absolute status of the individualistic "I." The world does not exist as a visual perspective to be conquered but rather as a surrounding field which englobes him and calls forth from him total participation in its reality. Neuronic Man lives in the group. The group is summed up in the image of the leader who is not a lonely Renaissance individual but a corporate figure, a myth, who sums up the dreams of those who participate in his life. The neuronic leader has no private life; more accurately, his private life is externalized and made public, as is the unconscious itself.

Elizabethan England ended with the personality --Walter Raleigh-- being executed by the non-personality, King James I. Neuronic Man may well end by being executed by his own gadgets, like the anti-hero of the experimental movie, *David Holzman's Diary,* who exists only when he is being filmed by his own cameras.

The rational man of the eighteenth century, on the contrary, mediated his most primitive emotions through the prism of ideology. He rationalized his most visceral responses. Comte, for example, fell in love with Madame Clotilde de Vaux, a woman years his junior. Her early death so struck him with grief that he felt it necessary to shift his allegiance from science to humanity, symbolized by the dead idol of his beloved. For Neuronic Man, however, every human attachment is fulfilled and then forgotten. Pepsi has a lot to give -- now! Like the drink in question, what is given is over, once consumed. Neuronic Man is never disappointed. Disappointment, as a human experience, demands a lively awareness of the difference between what is and what might have been. Anticipation, as a steadily entertained possibility for the future, is foreign to him. So too is disappointment, as a steadily entertained awareness of what might have been but will not be.

30

Total electronic participation in the rites of the image do not produce the heated-up totalitarianism of the Hitler Youth of forty years ago. Electronic participation gives us Al Monday, the cool jewel thief turned cop, and a new caper every Tuesday.

3 The Politics of Neuronic Man

Neuronic Man in the political order is not won over ultimately by issues.

Issues ultimately are reducible to drives located in man's other systems, be they physical or trans-physical. The nervous system never concentrates on anything. The nervous system is the concentrating. Its synthesizing product is the imaged field.

Statesmanship in the age of Neuronic Man will concentrate increasingly upon a field of images into which the voters can project whatever content they wish to. This is the secret of the masterpiece of Richard Milhous Nixon in Peking.

The empty airport, the quiet streets, the omnipresence of the bicycle, the absence of automobiles, the baggy pants and Mao, the sameness of men and women, the reserved and withdrawn politeness of Chou En-lai, the splendor of the snowy secret city, the Great Wall, the innumerable toasts, acupuncture, --into this, any imaginative man can read anything. It was the doing of an image, not the image of a doing. Its meaning will not emerge for another fifty years. But its significance for this moment in history consists in its having been done at all.

The summit at Peking constituted the coming of age of the new politics of Neuronic Man --Telepolitics.

4 Neuronic Identification

Conflicting interests locked in tension have historically cre-ated a balance that precluded internal disintegration. Today

31

these interests --thanks to their having been symbolized telepolitically-- heighten differences and thus harden them into neuronic opposites. Everybody turns inward towards his own group by tuning in on the tube and everybody does so at the expense of critical objectivity.

The masters of media do not desire neuronic identification. They do not know where it comes from any more than they can pinpoint the "cause" of violence in the streets. The Attica Prison riot was clearly a confrontation of white establishment jailers with alienated Black prisoners, but the media did all it could substantively to prevent this identification by a nation watching with horrified fascination the events at that hitherto little-known prison.

Busing school children to achieve a mythological "racial balance" in the fall of 1971 was presented as an unqualified success by television which insisted that the people had accepted, although reluctantly in many cases, the Supreme Court decision in favor of this tactic for producing racial integration. Busing, as the entire American people knew, was a dismal failure in September, 1971. It is probably television that made it fail. Because of television Blacks wanted no part of Whitey's school system. It was TV, after all, that let Blacks identify in "Black is beautiful! "

Broadcasters and television management still think in terms of "straight" reporting and of calling the shots as they are. But, in fact, broadcasters call the shots the way they see them, not the way they are.

Spiro Agnew has stood as an establishment watchdog during the Nixon Administration to see that the media behave objectively. We suggest that Mr. Agnew is absolutely right in all of his allegations against the news media, but for abso- lutely the wrong reasons. It is of the very nature of the news media to distort, if nothing else by what they decide to omit from reportage, thereby making it "not news." When the Attica riot showed Black against white clearly on the tube as medium and message, the doctoring of the evidence by news media analysts in terms of their own priority system came out as simple pleading for credibility in their creed.

The objectivity and impersonality consubstantial with an older science lingers on as part of a decaying creed which would both "tell it as it is" and see to it that things are getting better, that the sacred law of progress has not been abrogated. The intrinsic contradiction is compounded in that the overarching finality of television has little to do with reproducing or matching "external" reality.

Television creates a new reality. TV does not imitate nature by matching but by making something new. But this truth has been penetrated profoundly only by the makers of advertising and the managers of some telepolitical images. The Nixon of the men who masterminded his splendid media campaign in 1968 was the Nixon who, avoiding old-fashioned mass audiences, won the presidency.

After Joe McGinniss' devastating book, *The Selling of the President,* Richard Nixon had to demonstrate to the nation that he could speak live and unrehearsed over the medium. On January 2, 1972, he kicked off his first presidential campaign appearance in a live unrehearsed interview with Dan Rather, in which he brilliantly said nothing about everything. His appearance, live, was an anticipated counterattack to accusations of the necessity of staging in order for Richard Nixon to come through. The unstaged was carefully staged, a very formal informality indeed.

Television thus dovetails into a sensibility created by modern art insisting that art is more real than nature. As Henry James wrote: "It is art that makes life, makes interest, makes importance."

Neuronic identification does not follow on a televised report concerning tribes already in being.

33

Television creates these groups by abolishing space and time and by rendering possible an identification that cuts across national frontiers, linguistic barriers, and venerable ideological oppositions.

5 The Electronic Destruction of Tomorrow

An "ability to look ahead" required an effort; it set the person making the effort apart from those who could not or would not do so. The very act conferred superiority on the lonely, individual reader, and drew him into the dominant puritan work mystique which placed a premium on hard labor and looked upon life as essentially a pilgrimage from here to there. The bookworm was both hated and admired.

Participation with the distant in the electric age is produced altogether without visual imagination. The effects are massive. The image-exchange world has replaced the projected world of a promised tomorrow, except for the highly literate who sense increasingly that their culture is threatened by a new order of things. The image is externalized now by the lens of the "camera," * whereas it has been internalized in the past. The history of photography confirms this dramatically: traditionally, photographs in books and magazines have been used as illustrative of the text. Today an electronic reversal gives us written texts by the ton which study the film and televised image.

The broad extension of the two-dimensional visual imagination has been suspended in a youth which is highly impatient at school with long literary descriptive passages. Dickens is simply too slow for a generation weaned on the nano-second now. But even were the rapid time rhythms of today deliberately slowed down --and formal schooling does valiantly try to slow them down to late nineteenth century

* A television "camera" is not a camera in the strict sense of the photographic definition of the term.

34

rhythms-- young people could not warm to Victorian description. Those passages in Dickens and Scott and Thackeray
depended on a reading public that would visualize both
broadly and narrowly and turn a paragraph into a complex
picture in the imagination.

But the decay of visualization is not restricted to the young.
We find it everywhere in middle-aged and elderly people
whose sense ratios have been altered radically in the past
fifteen years. They cannot enjoy a written culture that
once was second nature to them. Are we moving into a
world without Walter Mittys whose timid external lives are
contradicted by worlds of wild adventures dreamed in the
secrecy of a private and interior chamber of the heart?
Today's Walter Mitty has even his dreams dreamed for him.

The electronic revolution would seem then to be an enemy
of ambiguity. Men tend to live more and more on the surface, thanks to their participation in the new realities of
image-exchanging. Critical faculties are thus suspended and
eventually atrophied in that no internal criteria can be used
with which to evaluate the televised world. Fantasy withers
because the difference between fantasy and reality is reduced.

Opposition between Black and white, rich and poor, students
and police, are produced as horizontal polarizations of
interiorized wars created externally by the juxtaposition
of hostile images. The return of costuming evidences the
new conviction among many young people that a man *is*
as he *seems.*

The older fantasies of the imagination become contemporary
realities. We are our masks and, in becoming them, the subconscious, discovered in the age of Freud, retreats back to
its Victorian origins. The mask, man's collective unconscious,
is now extended outwards, for all the world to see. Jung's
persona is turned inside out.

35

6 The Inner Trip

The inner drug trip might suggest a contradiction to the above but in fact the inner trip confirms our contention. The solipsistic and highly subjective cradling of the addict into his world of images is produced medicinally by an underground industry that preys on a youth whose imaginative faculties have been so dulled that, quite literally, no inner resources of the spirit and imagination can be called upon by those who would transcend the dreariness of reality. Today the child and non-child fantasize through pre-fantasized fantasies.

Three-dimensional TV advertising promises us an in-depth experience of the gorgeous blonde who emerges out of the screen to sit on your lap and promise you bliss if you buy this or that hair tonic. When electrodes which reproduce *all* perceptual experiences and synthesize them tactilely are hooked to the human skull, then we must ask ourselves why anybody would do anything for himself.

The science fiction morality tale of a future in which even the experience of sexual intercourse is induced electronically altogether without a human partner, is a technological probability. Rats have been so wildly delighted with pleasure created electronically that they have collapsed in exhaustion after having been subjected to better than 8,000 stimuli in a matter of minutes.

We must ask ourselves the truly frightening philosophical question: what is the reality of sailing a boat in a brisk wind; or getting drunk on port wine; or going to bed with a loved one? Is it, quite precisely, sailing the boat, getting drunk or going to bed? Or is it the *experience* of sailing the boat, getting drunk, or going to bed?

All experiences that man has known can today be duplicated electronically, except possibly the satisfaction of knowing that he has done the business himself. Chemistry even hopes to solve that problem.

But this last is not an image but a moral judgment. Moral judgments require an in-depth insight which always uses images but which are never reducible to them. Do we move inexorably towards an order of things in which meaning is feeling and feeling is being? For four hundred years the public orthodoxy of the West has been "I think, therefore I am." Will the first principle of a new age become: "I feel, therefore I am?"

Telepolitical identification is the union of a participant with prefabricated images projected by the electronic world of simultaneity. Reality is the image on the tube. The spectator, because of his need to "fill in" the image he sees on the screen, either becomes what is performed for him or he lives a schizophrenic life. Wernher von Braun tells us that he hopes to spend ten days on the moon within five years' time from this writing. Most people under thirty couldn't care less, because they have already been there.

The most significant fall-out of the space program is the lassitude and boredom with which youngsters greet every new moon landing. Only emergency conditions aboard the space vehicle galvanize the attention of earthmen, fascinated by the almost absurd contingent danger of beings as tiny and presumptuous as man, stranded helplessly in the vastness of space, with only the invisible umbilical cord of electronically moving information connecting them to "home," the "good earth."

To a Von Braun, to a man who planned the landings from Houston, the possibility of going from earth to moon retains its Jules Verne charm. But then Von Braun is not a product of the age he helped create. Born and bred in an older order of things, Von Braun senses the crack-through into outer space as a liberation of man from the confines of this earth. But the rim-spin of our planet by electronic techno-

37

logy has worked an inner contradiction into the heart of
mankind which has reacted, not by celebrating a liberation,
but by experiencing the secret dread that comes out of an
awareness of total contingency and loneliness. Buckminster
Fuller's Space-Ship Earth, as well as the lonely astronaut's
"good earth," point to a sense of constriction.

Hemmed in by our own electronic technology which has
willy-nilly surrounded us in a Chardinian videosphere;
panicked by the conviction that the older mechanical
technology has so raped the cosmos that we must exist
from thence until the end as men staving off an inevitable
disaster; turned into shepherds of being whose flock is too
numerous for the narrow and exhausted resources of the
earth, men escape into an imaged world which demands
total participation, hence identification. We must all be
as we seem!

Countermovements attest to the panic. Jesus Freaks seek
salvation in non-institutional religion. The Satanic cults
along the broad Pacific coast of California, and throughout
the land, would chain the forces of good and evil by
celebrating the Faustian dimension of human existence.
Everyone frantically seeks security in something. There
are those who wish to flee politically into the past. Gripped
powerfully by the old puritan ethic that still haunts the
backwaters of the American spirit, the reactionaries in our
midst --and they number into the tens of millions-- are
uneasy with the new technology. This is true of Jesus
Freaks, Panthers, Communists, Encounter Groups, new
Satanists, "commune" dwellers and hippies. They reject it
or use it awkwardly. The frantic search for security often
takes the form of flight into the outdoors. The investment of
millions in sports goods and other leisure industries attests
to a desperate need to go somewhere else, to be where we
are not now.

Buttressed by the new media which both report these events
and further them by the lure of advertising, these counter-

movements of the psyche are deeply hostile to the telepolitical world because they suggest that *reality is not the
image of the world* and that a simulated adventure around
the world is no adventure at all. But the fact is that
the man who does go around the world once every night
does so at home as he gets the image of the reality from
his set. That image is the new reality and it does really
move him to go around the world (and also to buy whatever
is advertised).

7 The End of Objectivity

The obvious and conventional objection is made, upholding
"objectivity in reporting" which is presumed to be the glory
of a free press. But in truth there can be no more objectivity
in a newscast than in a Broadway comedy. If the "truth"
of television reporting is considered to be a matching of
reality reported, with events as they occurred, then television
must be written off as a colossal lie. A type of television
vérité is impossible because of the discontinuity and juxtaposition of all televised content inside the iconic TV form.

Synthesizing sixteen hours of footage into a thirty to sixty
minute newscast is a creative act.

The "product" is *not* the news as it happened today.
The product is the artistic creation of reporters, editors,
newscasters, technicians, and sponsors who assemble a
montage of images. These images --through selection or
omission, emphasis or lack of emphasis, through the
progression of the imaged sequences in which they are
placed, through the locale in which they are to be viewed--
totally transcend the myth of objectivity and "honest"
reporting. The professional "cutters" and "pasters"
of the major networks are not hypocrites when they raise
aloft the banner of objectivity. They are simply naive.

They are innocent about the essential artistry and wizardry
of their own magical profession.

News reporting is biased by its very nature. It could exist no other way. Every synthetic act of mind and sensibility transcends the content that goes into it. A so-called news "analysis" is really a "synthesis." A Walter Cronkite newscast is as creative an act as is the layout of the front page of a major newspaper. Synthesis is another word for creativity. Both have to do with making, not matching. The effect is not that which occurred in the real world. The effect *is* a world.

Or, more precisely, the effect is a bewildering dust of new worlds, themselves the satellites of electronic rim-spin. We will be arguing throughout these pages that Telepolitics is not leading the more advanced technologically-developed nations into monolithic totalitarianism, but into neuronic differentiation. Each neuron has its own "truth." So, too, does each communication system.

8 The Return of the Barbarians

Today barbarism returns with a vengeance. Even the beards and long hair suggest Vikings falling upon the north of England. Woodstock is as barbarian as was ninth century Denmark.

But the differences are more crucial than the likenesses. The collapse of the Roman order and the return of Europe to the darkness of the forests in those wild centuries preceding the coming of Charlemagne were not the work of men escaping civilization. The tribes were always trying to get inside the Empire, to eat the fruit they had not tended. They were wild children who knew nothing and wanted everything --- for nothing! They learned eventually that to enjoy the fruit they had to tend the vine.

Today these new primitives emerge from out of the heart of civilization and they find it wanting. They want to destroy machines in economics, restore mystery in religion, exalt blood in culture. Impatient of the elaborate rules of society,

they want instantaneous sex with neither prior preparation
nor posterior responsibility for consequences; they want all
problems solved right now --wars ended, poverty abolished,
inequalities leveled. Despising liberal capitalism and the
puritan ethic upon which it reposes, they land in Luxembourg
on Icelandic Airlines and crawl through a shocked Europe,
shabby and dirty boys and girls, pretending to a poverty
they have never known, strangely reminiscent of thirteenth
century Franciscans.

More serious primitives, such as the Panthers and Black
Muslims, stay home and impose a fierce puritanism upon
their members as they train for the moment of glory.
Were we to seek a historical parallel, we would find one, not
in the blond barbarians from the north scrambling over the
ill-defended frontiers of the Roman Empire, but in the flight
of the desert monks to the east and away from the city, a
flight that marked the decaying centuries of Imperial rule
before the blackout, or in the Islamic embrace of simplicity
in religion and complexity in marriage that exploded in
one lone cavalry charge through the north of Africa,
leaving the wells dry and the cities empty, and giving the
Magreb to the sands.

9 Massive Ignorance and Planned Violence

Despising the computer, the answers of the new barbarians
today mirror the computer's robot-like ignorance of
reflection and responsibility. Espousing liberty, they do not
know that their own tribal life is more authoritarian than
anything that they react against. Preaching sexual liberation, they create families more rigid than those from which
they came. There is something macabre about the constant
reference by the press to the Manson gang as the "Manson
family." Formed of three young women and two young
men who fled conventional family life, they were told
to "Kill, kill, kill! " by their "Father." A milder
authority uncertain of itself yielded to a pathological

41

authority secure in the depths of its being: the Manson girls did not betray their leader and dynastic father.

Remembering democracy only as a slogan, the new primitives anneal themselves from within, thanks to a savage tribal loyalty under dynastic chieftains. Chavez, marching under the Fresno sun with revolutionary priests carrying banners of the Virgin of Guadalupe, crying out for justice for his own, understands these things. There is probably no tribe in America that abominates more thoroughly the Satanic tribes found throughout the south of California celebrating their black masses over the bodies of prostitutes, than do the sun-scorched *braceros* who burn out their youth bending low over grapes demanding ministration. These two tribes have nothing in common. There are sob sisters in neither. Barbarism sunders as does a sword. The neuronic tribes --all of them-- hate one another with a deep hate.

What do American Mexicans have in common with American Blacks? Literally, nothing at all! Perhaps they ought to have a communion of the oppressed, as they once had common brotherhood under a transcendent God. But the electronic age has ended the first, just as secularization has ended the second. The division cuts through all loyalties that once united; they do not even have the community of allegiance to a national state or the ideal of abstract equality of citizenship.

We have traveled a long way from the eighteenth century. Some try to play the game of the system and try to get their members to register and vote. They might prefer to do the job with guns if they had enough hands to outshoot the WASP establishment.

But the presuppositions of "the System" reject its being used for something presumed to be more profound and ultimate than itself!

Traditional American democracy agreed that minorities
simply *had to* buckle under once their erstwhile opponents
had made their cause the law of the land. Even the South
accepted, albeit reluctantly, the victory of the North in
the Civil War. This acceptance --so thoroughly American--
is incredible in a European context. The Spanish left,
for example, began to conspire against the Franco victory
the day his Nationalist troops marched triumphantly into
Madrid. But in the U.S.A. we believe in fair play. Or we did!

10 Media: Outside or Inside

Urbanized man increasingly lives inside an electronic world
uniting him with everyone in space even as it tends toward
the obliteration of time as hitherto understood. Social
critics such as Gabiel Marcel in his *Man Against Mass Society,*
and Gustave Thibon in his *Retour au Réel* have noted the
removal of nature from the forefront of human consciousness and nature's replacement by the world of television.

The calculations taken to put two men on the moon almost
totally escape both observation and vizualization. Most of
the overseers of the whole operation cannot *see,* even imagine,
what they are doing. The tragic effects of the new order have
been explored sufficiently in Marcel, Thibon, Picard, Pieper
and others. It suffices simply to enumerate them: the
removal of man from natural springs of piety; the confusion
between what is the real world and what is ersatz; the decay
of genuine conversation in the home, the emptiness of man's
head as his brain merely imitates the electronic world outside; the constantly-repeated commercial lie that there
is an answer to every human problem; the terrible loneliness
of being seated hour after hour before television after a
day's work and knowing everyone in the world and being
known to no one. We need not labor these points. They
find their objective correlative in the awesome silence of
the lunar surface.

To deplore is one act. To pretend that man has not entered a new order of being, for good or evil, is something else again. The evolutionists among us are given the lie here. Man did not *evolve* into the electronic world. He was catapulted into it.

It follows that any attempt to deal with the politics of media, Telepolitics, as though politics were *here* and media *there,* is doomed to failure, tricked by a sleight of hand of the visual imagination. Only the "anonymous observer" of the older mechanical world could plausibly come to grips with electronics in this fashion. But Werner Heisenberg, philosophizing in the name of the new physics, some time ago laid the ghost of the anonymous observer to rest when he pointed out that in modern scientific theory no one knows where nature begins and man lets off. Analogously, no one knows where man --the observer of media-- lets off and man --created in the image of the media-- commences. A grave and ancient philosophical problem returns again to the forum of the human spirit. What, after all, is real and what is illusion? No one really knows any more.

The Chicago convention of 1968 illustrated this confusion between illusion and reality. Millions of television watchers were better informed about what was going on in Convention Hall than were the individual delegates themselves.

The convention revealed its dinosaur quality in that the older mechanical principle of the chain of command was observed. Chairmen caucused with their delegations, attempted to parlay their influence with representatives of the major candidates, came to decisions and passed down instructions in the traditional fashion. The essence of any chain of command is its taking *time,* moving from decisions arrived at above to instructions passed on below and finally action --in this case, voting. The television audience was aware of top-level decisions long before the individual delegates on the floor were informed of them. Transistor radios could be seen pressed to delegates' ears. They were trying to stay abreast of what was *really* happening. The whole comedy was succinctly noted by an obscure delegate from one of the Great Plains states who wiped his brow in disgust at the end of the first day's proceedings, expostulating: "I'm going back to my hotel to get four hours' sleep and find out in tomorrow's newspaper what the whole nation knows tonight and what we don't know yet. What the hell did we do today anyway? "

11 Disappearing Privacy

Old-fashioned politics is a mixture of altruism, self-interest, wheeling and dealing, and a give-and-take carried on within the secrecy of smoke-filled rooms.

Chicago taught us that logical contradictions can walk around the world even if they cannot do so inside the human mind. Old-fashioned politics demands secrecy. There was secrecy *inside* Convention Hall, but this secrecy was known to everybody *outside* Convention Hall. This is somewhat analogous to sex secretly performed by a man and woman who are simultaneously watched through a keyhole. Putting the older political order on television is pornographic. It does not abolish that order, any more than lions in a zoo seen through bars by children are abolished. Yet no one would suggest that lions in a zoo are the same as lions in the jungle. The 1968 election turned the American institution of the political convention into a zoo!

Television did for America what Evelyn Waugh once suggested with tongue-in-cheek the socialist government do with the English aristocracy: put some of the disappearing specimens in an enormous park centered by a country house, surrounded by hounds and scarlet-coated gentlemen and ladies riding side-saddle, making thus a picturesque and free spectacle for the millions of proletarians who looked in from outside. Waugh's irony, the product of the years immediately following World War II, has been made reality by mass electronic media. Chain-of-command politics

45

involves old-fashioned space and time decisions made *here* and *now* and passed on to subordinates who are *there!*

The abolition of space and time electronically destroys secrecy. Politics has become once again as public as it was in the age of the Sun King, Louis XIV. We need only think of the massive public speculation concerning what Senator Kennedy was up to on that fateful night on the Chappaquidick bridge, or of the insistence that Eagleton should have told all details of his hospital sojourns. Peripherally this means that nobody can get away with anything anymore. Centrally it means that everything political of significance is staged on media, better yet, *inside* media. Politics has become a show.

Privacy exists, of course, but whereas those centuries immediately preceding the electronic revolution saw privacy ever advancing in proportion to a man's ascendancy in the scale of power, privacy today is ever decreasing in exact proportion to the same ascendancy toward power.

America's putting astronauts on the moon was publicly staged from its inception through to its spectacular execution with re-entry, splashdown, and the President of the United States joking with "our men" in their quarantine cage. Every word uttered by Armstrong, Aldrin and Collins was noted by the whole world. A favorite game sprang up in the days preceding the launching of Apollo 11. What would be the first words said by man on the moon? An almost archaic and stiff symbolism clustered around and covered every gesture and romp over the moon's surface by "our men." Mrs. Madeleine Murray O'Hare filed a court suit, insisting that future astronauts refrain from following the example of the crew of Apollo 10 who merrily read Scripture and dispensed electronic Christmas cards to the earth 250,000 miles away. Mrs. Murray O'Hare insists that this is a violation of the treasured doctrine of separation of church and state.

Astronauts praying or not praying belong now to the public order. Their every gesture has become corporate ritual. Therefore groups and individuals, lusting after the public incarnation of *their* vision of the real, jostle for position in a game whose end is converting moonflyers into political marionettes.

12 Moon and Mars Dancing

Moon and Mars dancing may be the liturgy of tomorrow, possibly as boring to tomorrow's youth as is the latter day liturgical dancing in our churches to everyone today. The career of an astronaut has become symbolic of the newer political order. No one on the moon can do anything privately. Alone on that desolate surface the astronaut is known to every man on earth. Enjoying and suffering solitude, he is utterly without privacy.

The conquest of the moon was the most public event history has ever known. And it was precisely the conquest of the most distant, lonely and solitary geographical surface that man has seen.

The astronauts are not only a symbol. They mark the advent of a new reality.

This reality, Telepolitics, simply cannot be domesticated by reducing the new technics to a merely linear advancement or progression upon the older. Something new has happened to man. He has entered into an order of existence which has radically transformed *his relationship with his fellow-man.* Man's relationship with man, after all, is the most profound understanding of politics that the entire philosophical tradition of the West has thus far elaborated.

13 The Return of the Spoken Myth

Political propaganda, whose master in the immediate past was Dr. Joseph Goebbels, is a return of the mythic, therefore

47

a return of the dominance of the oral. The oral tradition, even as it has survived in the East and in pockets within the West, is the enemy of the two counterpoints within the movement of politics within the past several centuries: the romantic and the progressive.

Although both traditions have been at war with one another in our civilizations, both constitute --so to speak-- the thesis and anti-thesis out of which there was woven the synthesis of modern civilization. Romanticism was the spur which created the vast body of historical scholarship done by men who were dedicated to the ideal of impartial objectivity.

The genius of good historiography involved the capacity to skip over the present and repose in the past. This discipline was, of course, the product of high literacy. Projection backwards, first done romantically, was then disciplined into historical objectivity.

But the mythological, the neuronic, springs of propaganda, make the deeds of the past a kind of perpetual present or now. In primitive societies the role has always belonged to the teller of tales who obliterates time and objectifies distance.

The teller of tales, the seer, was a precursor of the electronic. Both block any effective understanding of past as distant from present. Both check the romantic skipping over time backwards, the historian's "space" required for the coolness of judgment, *and* the progressive leap into an idealized future. Romanticism and progressivism are muted within the electronic world.

Mythologically the whole of history moves around us in the now. Ours is the most historical of all ages. Every moment of history is present at the press of a button or the turn of a dial to contemporary man. Roman togas jostle with Edwardian waistcoats. Plato and Heidegger sit at the same table, often with Krishna and Lao-tse.

48

Eastern beads are rattled and Eastern robes are worn and
Eastern incense is burned in the streets of Berkeley and
televised via satellite to Tokyo. Viking hairdos are commonplace in banks. More is known about King Richard III of
England today than was known thirty years after his death.
The magic of the movie makes Waterloo a more vivid
panorama than it was to any of its participants. We know
more about the seventh century's introduction of the
stirrup into the West than did men of the eighth century.
There is no longer any past. Every past is a present wardrobe
whose garments are to be put on at will. An environment of
total information is an englobing historical wraparound.
In a frightening vision of existence even the dawn of creation
returns with the burnt-out craters of the moon.

Simultaneously, things happen so rapidly that they are a
past before we have even conceived them as a future. "Future
shock" is a misnomer. If the future is now and the past is
now, what has happened to the dynamism of change? *What*
is changing and *where* is the continuum of change?

Youngblood insists that change is a global constant, our
only global constant, which suggests Juenger's thesis that
the perfection of anything, in this case change, is its
destruction.

The tragedy of contemporary man is in part his inability
either to react backwards or progress forwards. Both past
and future are an electronic now. Frozen in a simultaneity
of images, change has become the discontinuous appearance
and disappearance of world after world of images. In such
a merry-go-round man can only seize the rung of the
ersatz horse as it passes him by on the screen, mount a
simulated saddle and fit himself to unreal stirrups on a
ride which whirls him round and round until what was once
solid earth becomes a distant and dizzying vortex of unreal
fantasies.

Part II
The Neuronic Age

1 The Revolution is Over

Ni la réalité de Jésus, ni la réalité de Marx, mais la réalité de la télévision!

Neither the reality of Jesus nor the reality of Marx, but the reality of television. The Revolution is Over!

No one seriously doubts but that the older American order is in full decay. According to French writer Jean-François Revel,* the new world revolution will break out in the United States of America. We radically challenge the thesis of *Without Marx or Jesus* that the new world revolution will take place, or is taking place, in America. We say it already *has* taken place. What M. Revel outlines so perceptively as *causes* of a new world revolution, the authors of this study consider to be a valid description of *effects* of a revolution already aging by electronic time criteria.

Revel sees America splintered into at least three predominant tribes: the Black "Nation," the Woodstock "Nation," and the Wallace "Nation." To these tens of millions, possibly a fifth of America's population, there are added Women's Liberation, Gay Liberation, the emerging Chicano "Nation,"

* *Without Marx or Jesus,* trans. J.F. Bernard (N.Y:Doubleday, 1971)

51

and a rapidly growing Indian "Nation" that briefly
occupied Alcatraz. Some of these tribes cross one another
in that a Women's Liberationist can belong to the Woodstock
tribe and a Gay Liberationist can make common cause with
the goals of Women's Liberation. But the hostile lines of
internal self-identification are hardening.

The going Establishment, certainly a numerical majority in
the early seventies, not only finds it difficult to govern this
dust of alien and conflicting groups but suffers the temptation to tribalize itself in an automatic gesture of self-
defense, to defuse the revolution by absorbing as many
of its symbols and causes as possible, to keep open its doors
to members of the Woodstock "Nation" who wish to drop
back in as the enthusiasms of youth wear off with the years.

The Jesus Freaks tribe poses a threat to the frank paganism of
the Woodstock tribe because the Jesus Freaks have adopted
all the external symbolism, the language, and the music of
the youth revolution, while bending them to an amorphous
Christianity which is open to any kind of doctrinal formu-
lation because of its very vagueness. The Freaks are also a
threat to fundamentalist Protestant churches of the Establishment because the Freaks reject the middle-class and
puritan cultural ethos associated with these communions.

Billy Graham's wooing of the Jesus People and his frank
praise for their sincere religiosity is a striking instance of
the Establishment's attempt to broaden its base by ingesting
whatever it can of its enemies. We are reminded of Rome's
policy of conferring citizenship on alien tribes and thus
absorbing them within the Empire. The policy worked
admirably until the absorbed tribes outnumbered their
hosts and thus gradually barbarized Roman civilization.

There is, in short, a cutoff point in the tactic of adoption
and absorption. Beyond that point, the Establishment would
cease to be what it is: America with its liberal and conservative and moderate tendencies, composed --in the last analysis--

of men and women who consider themselves to be, ultimately, American citizens of a classical nation state and not tribesmen principally loyal to this or that faction.

Walker Percy in *Love in the Ruins* has middle America living in highly technologized and super modern suburbs equipped with hospitals and rest homes for the aged, golf courses, and country clubs. This America is cut off from the rest of the country which is filled with decaying Howard Johnson restaurants lying along abandoned super-highways and drive-in theaters covered over with vines as nature returns to retrieve its primeval dominance. This is the post-auto age in which bearded youths and a Black Bantu nation live in forests and menace the fortress suburbs of middle America, itself divided internally into conservative and liberal. It is an age some twenty to thirty years hence when everyone has a gun on everyone else. The dramatic irony is that the projection is already here.

The Praetorians have emerged in order to prevent this return to barbarism.

2 The Praetorian Alternative --The Pentagon and the Right Wing

Praetorians neither invent nor restore. Their role in history is to conserve what has been or is thought still to be. The Praetorian is the hero of the long holding action, as were those French parachute units in Indochina and later under Salan in Algeria who represented a defense of French civilization even after that very civilization had made its peace with the Algerians.

The most likely candidates for a Praetorian holding action to the rapidly disintegrating situation in the United States are the Pentagon and the right wing whose paladin at this moment is George Wallace. But the Pentagon could not play the role of avenging savior by itself. Despite its possession of a magnificent communications system, which is

53

independent of the media of the Establishment, the Pentagon lacks --down in the ranks-- the esprit needed to act on its own initiative.

Attacked by both Establishment media and the New Left, the Pentagon faces the appalling truth that its own military units are riddled with doubts and drugs. Its junior officers are fragged in Vietnam. Attacked by an unseen enemy from without and a seen enemy from within, the officer corps and the old line regular army sergeants --always America's military backbone in every war she has fought, according to General "Black Jack" Pershing-- have withdrawn into themselves. Sensing the frustration of not being permitted to win, englobed by a deeper paradox of what "winning" is anymore, America's professional soldiers approach although they do not yet reach, the frustration of the French parachute troops and the Legion in North Africa in the late fifties.

The Praetorian guard has historically been the conversion of soldiers into cops. Two United States Air Force F-111 jets tracking commercial airline hijackers over northern Colorado (January 20, 1970) and announcing publicly the availability of their services for future hijacking escapades portends a possible coming domestic Praetorian solution A huge military industrial complex does not simply disappear because the nation dissolves into conflicting tribes. Geared to act, this complex must *do* something. Denied victory abroad, this complex might very well seek compensation by victory within.

Obscurely aware that the patience of the military may not be as long-lasting as Job's, the Government quietly eliminates crack units such as the Green Berets. Another tribe --and one armed to the teeth-- will not be tolerated by a political order whose broad base is a citizenry whose way of life is under attack from all sides and whose deepest aspiration is to survive with what it now possesses, with or without honor.

An alliance between the Pentagon and the Right, the night-mare of contemporary liberalism, would require that both Pentagon and the right wing cease believing in law. But law is God to both. A Praetorian revolution would have to deny its own theology. Its theology is law, not revolution.

The military adores the new electronic technology. Their potential allies on the Right do not. The right wing in America loathes the new world produced by media because they think it is the enemy of what they love. They have reason to despise television because television has been the principal cause of the tribalization and atomization threatening their cherished American Right -- be it the phalanx of Governor Wallace or the right wing within the conventional two parties.

The Right does not consider itself to be a "nation" or a tribe. It believes sincerely that it stands for America and Americanism. In making this claim apodictically, however, the Right identifies America with a specific set of political doctrines and excommunicates those who do not take communion at this table of truth. Thus the Right tribalizes itself and identifies fiercely with its own.

A tribe is identified ultimately by its temptation toward secession from the whole system.

3 The Underground Press and the Passing of Print

Man's psyche is rarely satisfied by crusades against what everyone considers to be sin, such as war and poverty. The daimonic must be concretized and even personalized. Black concretizes evil in Whitey; Redneck concretizes evil in revolution; in turn these national and generic identifications are further personalized in individuals: Tim Leary, Rap Brown, the Berrigan brothers, Caesar Chavez, Richard Nixon, Spiro Agnew, George Wallace. The underground press thus gives scope to this dark but essential dimension of the human spirit.

55

The Establishment is still, obscurely at least, the heir to the traditions of the Enlightenment, of the Age of Reason. Commentators Smith and Sevareid and Brinkley exude an air of sweet reasonableness as they appeal, or seem to appeal, to man's better self. A direct attack on the viscera is not respectable. But the form of television invades the viscera directly and the reason only concurrently. Mr. Huntly urges a rational solution to the Vietnam war and seconds later Schlitz sends you around the world --you only go around once, you know! -- with a can of beer in your hand. There is a form-content war even *on* the TV screen itself.

But the underground press finds villains and heros everywhere, men to love and hate. It seeks incarnations for profoundly human daimonic drives. These latter-day hot-gospelers are decidedly non-rationalist, non-Cartesian, non-enlightened. Yet, ironically, print was the formal mode that spread rationalism throughout the West.

Is print ending as it began? In those first years following Gutenberg's invention, printed pamphlets and books-- heretical bibles and inflammatory tracts against the going order-- were passed from hand to hand by men who were persecuted by the going establishment, then an orally-structured establishment.

Is print ending as it began by grinding out angry tracts in obscure basement presses in the name of a New Protest? Will a new electronic establishment end with its own Inquisition?

Print may very well, indeed, die in basements where little underground presses churn out the bitterness and frustration of their owners.

Students of media have failed almost universally to take into account the rapid mushrooming into existence of this subterranean world, itself composed of media: cheaply printed books, pamphlets, underground press, newsletters, flyers. The movement is too young to be evaluated definitively but it is precisely what the word "movement" suggests: "On the move." The underground changes weekly, if not daily, and it is impossible to slot into predigested categories.

Representing all the bickering and irritation endemic to small groups forced to rub shoulders with fellow "saints" day after day, these knots of the discontented spend more time shivering lances against their own members than against the enemy and they tend to reproduce themselves by osmosis. This quicksilver of little magazines and underground papers is occasionally noted by establishment media, but the quicksilver itself can never be pinned to the wall of strict categorization.

4 The Respectable Revolution

Is the nation being so polarized that only the extremes talk to one another, in strident language over hushed media, while the mainstream talks to nobody but itself, over strident media in "hushed" terms?

The hushed pablum that passes for conversation on the talk shows is controlled by a code of etiquette more rigid than that of the Byzantine court. Comedians and starlets interlard their compliments on each other's last successful five-week engagement at the Sahara or the hungry i with observations on race problems, war and peace, and other conundrums with the clownish imputation that these issues constitute their major concern. Agents cluck affirmatively from the wings. Johnny and Merv nod their heads and adjust their ties because just the right thing has been said at just the right time. The total conventionality of it all, often in the name of respectable unconventionality, is both banal and reassuring. The audience gets what it expects, identifies with "greatness," goes to sleep in order to arise the following day remembering not a word of what was said, but assuaged all the more in knowing that its world is as it was and will be.

The bitterness and profound alienation, the sundering swords dividing those who engage in underground media politics from establishmentarian television and press, is compounded of part envy and part contempt; envy for being denied access to the road to power and glory, contempt for the putative banality that passes for wisdom on these same media.

Nonetheless, the Establishment has shown itself remarkably clever and even Machiavellian in its ability to defuse underworld political and social pressures by inviting their spokesmen to participate in the great televised conversation.

In this way even Black Panther leaders have been conventionalized. To become a familiar figure on the talk show circuit is far more effective castration than the silence piously willed by Spiro Agnew. Afro hair wigs, initially symbols of protest against white culture, are worn by the most conventional of Black sportscasters. Peace symbols are seen at black tie affairs. Long hairs become cops on *Mod Squad.* A Black hoodlum rises to be the righthand man of *Ironsides.* Rebellious young lawyers find justice for their clients in the courts of the hated Establishment. Black clerks wear long sideburns, and sideburns are also quite popular today within the ranks of the grim conservative Young Americans for Freedom.

Symbols of rebellion are thus rendered respectable by the custodians of order.

5 Telepolitical Castration

Acceptance by American television --be it in fictional form, through advertising, newscasting or chitchat-- "establishes" the revolutionary by making him part of the image world, a familiar prop in the scenery commented on by Dick, Johnny and Merv.

Any future for the underground is predicated on its willingness to either seize the media or endure poverty. Since the former is a practical impossibility, only poverty remains as a viable alternative. One is reminded of Francisco Franco's political genius in cutting the entrails of political opposition in Spain by giving cabinet posts, and hence responsibilities, to men bent on destroying his regime.

The underground of both Left and Right have a future provided they remain "under" and "anonymous" to the media. "Hot" revolution must remain off the cool medium of television.

Who is more a part of the going liberal establishment in the United States than its highly televised critic, the conservative Mr. William F. Buckley, Jr.? What would the gadfly do if the house blew away? He would be a Socrates without Athens.

When the opposition --be it the "Revolution of Reaction" or of a leftist agnostic "Tomorrow"-- is put on television, it enters a new order of being. The revolution progressively ceases to be what it was and becomes something new, an imaged fantasy of the electronic world.

6 Wars: On and Off the Tube

Television flashes bloody wars on the screen of the human consciousness and homemakers are racked by guilt in viewing a world in flames in the coziness of their family rooms and dens.

But there is a great abyss in the political order, between the wars that are "on" and the wars that are "off." Ireland and, reluctantly, Biafra were "on" the media: even the dead in the streets of Belfast and in the African jungles were conferred the laurel of having once existed. But who hears of the unending civil wars in the Sudan (the recent announcement that a truce had been reached caused many a TV watcher

59

to exclaim: "I didn't even know there was a war on there.") or the Ukraine? These wars, as bloody as those televised, have been denied existence within the new order.

The politics that is not "on" belongs to another order of reality, as distinct from Telepolitics as are those silent gang wars in big city slums, ending with throats slit in dark alleys, from the peace and quiet of an upper middle-class suburb.

In some cases the masters of media simply do not know about the warring and whoring world beyond their own. This ignorance produces bitterness and indignation in the ignored. In other cases the masters of media know what happens beyond the media but either do not think the events are important enough to report, or suppress them because they embarrass ideological priorities. This attitude also produces bitterness and indignation in the ignored.

A new version of the ancient plot theory of history is being bred thoughout the nation. "They" know and "they" control the world!   And "they" have suppressed us by silencing our message and even our sacrifices unto death!

7 The Bias of Priorities

Politicians are often convinced that the difference between shaking hands down on the farm, issuing pronunciamentos in the local weekly, passing out handbills on the greensward of the state capital or entering the telepolitical world is a difference simply of degree and not of kind.

Two flaws mar this perfectly sensible conclusion: (1) electronic media create realities much better than they report them; (2) the masters of media --themselves only partially aware of the awesome power under their control-- adhere to hierarchies of priorities about ultimate goodness and truth. They may mask these convictions under the guise of impartial reporting but in fact they impose rigid

60

prejudgments upon all movements that vie for illumination under the glare of the electronic movement of information.

The *Early Morning Show* will entertain the opinions of a priest of Satan; the old Jack Paar show paraded a masked couple who belonged to a wife-swapping club. Ex-priests and ex-nuns, the vasectomized and the aborted, tell us how it was with them. Even murderers are interviewed in depth on the sadistic details of their crimes. But what you won't find discussed is the shabbiness of consumer products, the lack of nutrition in our foods, the threat to freedom of enterprise of conglomerates, or the threat to national states in multi-national corporations. These --and the problem of this book, the moral, cultural and political implications of TV itself-- the networks will not touch. And yet such problems ought to be very close to their liberal humanist stance.

Television is, of course, creating its politics, in which a rigid code dominates the permitted and the forbidden.

Telepolitics, like all politics everywhere and in all times, sets down its own ground rules for discussion. Acceptance, therefore, of the conditions for telepolitical discussion defines the man and the movement. But once so defined, the media have a capricious power to drop or to exalt. If dropped --as so many heros of the New Left have been dropped-- then the movement and its men sink into oblivion, to emerge, if ever, like Rap Brown shot down while attempting a cheap holdup. Politicians existing outside the electronic order are advised, therefore, to remain where they are if they are not willing to take the risks involved in entering. The emoluments if one enters successfully are, of course, obvious.

8 The Totalitarian Question

A rigid set of priorities governs television in the United States.

An implicit ethics concerning what is important and what
is not is accepted innocently by the broadcasters and
programmers, writers and actors. Within this ethic, broad
disagreement and even spirited opposition are permitted.
Answers are not dictated. *It is the questions that are
totalitarian.*

The same range of questions is reflected in talk shows, news
coverage, documentaries and educational TV. This new
morality cannot be defined with any ideological rigor. Such
a definition would dissolve the whole business in a sea of
marshmallows. Strength here lies in a vague mistiness
surrounding a hierarchy of concerns that are accepted as
absolutes: Our inner cities must be saved. Poverty has to be
eliminated. The standard of living for all peoples must go up.
Social Security must be increased, medical care nationalized,
problems of welfare solved. Education must be bigger and
better. Tensions between religions are to be erased and
eventually eliminated. These beads within a rosary form
the religion of the new Telepolitics. Behind these desiderata
--the list above is merely suggestive-- lies advertising's
implicit premise that there is a solution to every problem
to which flesh is heir.

When an older technology or medium or style of life ceases
to be, it becomes a symbolic figure or content for newer
technical media. The form of the nineteenth century was
the iron age of paleolithic industrialization. Simultaneously
its symbolic content was the age of Romanticism. Obsolescent forms return to society to take their vengeance as
symbolic dreams. Men will siphon off into fantasy the
content of their older environment. McLuhan, in commenting on violence on television, observed that all of the
collective fantasies of imaged violence could hardly begin
to match the substantial daily violence of the internal
combustion engine and its multi-level cultural effects.

Televised advertising symbolically re-iterates all of the
mechanical determinism of the older machine technology:

buy X and Z result will follow. The understanding of the relationship between causes and effects is totally linear and deterministic. Problems are set up and solutions are dis - covered. (No one seems to note that the solution is discovered first and the problem is subsequently invented.)

The content of the half hour and hour weekly dramas such as *Ironsides, Dragnet, Bonanza, Gunsmoke,* et al set forth problems, often of an enormous scope which we then solve within a matter of minutes. The problem-solving machine works itself out in religion where the Jesus Freaks movement, apparently fanatically opposed to industrialization, none- theless turns its God into a machine who mechanically guarantees salvation once he has been accepted. Jesus becomes, in fact, a *Deus ex machina!*

Truly heightened in advertising's implicit promise to solve all problems is television's list of totalitarian questions. In opposition to the discontinuity of the electronic form itself, these questions truly remain television's content. This content, we reiterate again, is the user of the medium, the master and the mastered.

Any political movement which does not place these problems to the forefront of its platform will not speak through the new media as now constituted.

Let it be noted carefully that the movement in question need not be *against* the new morality. The very generality of the telepolitical concerns is such that few people can intelli- gently oppose its projects, such as saving cities or healing poverty. A movement simply has to focus the thrust of its interest someplace else; has to advocate another hierarchy of goals to be achieved; has to give its deeper love to something new --or old-- for it to fail the test of telepolitical respectability. Failure here means silence in the new order of things.

Anyone who chooses not to go out into the desert has only one defense against television's totalitarian questions. He can try to understand what is happening to him, and this gives him a small advantage over those who do not know anything is at stake.

What happens to the poor non-conformist who refuses either to own a set or to watch television at all? What are the effects of the totalitarian questions on such a person? He is doomed to be influenced and manipulated blindly by an environment of questions which he will not understand on principle and with which he cannot cope in fact.

9 Silence as a Weapon

Television's concerns avalanche the viewer and his priorities. To be concerned about other things is to be resoundly silent on the new media. This silence creates the new order even as it distorts the old in failing to report it "as it is" or "was."

It is axiomatic in politics that action grows out of conviction and that convictions are part of reality. But the media as established cannot come to grips with convictions that fall outside of its own set of priorities.

The violent anti-busing emotions on the part of both Black and white find their only outlet in the symbolized fantasies of an Archie Bunker in *All in the Family.* The same can be said of the new poor white class of our cities, caught between emerging Black Power and a disappearing white middle class. Instances could be multiplied indefinitely. The student disenchanted with nineteenth century educational forms is denied any TV voice. So too is the political scientist who feels it's time to stop sentimentalizing about the virtues of small new national states and to take an unwavering look at the implications of Biafra, East Pakistan, and Uganda. The TV networks are too busy with other commitments.

One telepolitical concern that overwhelms the media today
is the conviction that the world is suffering from over-
population. Granting a broad spectrum of alternative means
for coming to grips with a burgeoning population problem,
television will both stage and report debates on the relative
merits of the pill, vasectomy, abortion, periodical abstinence,
and other contraceptive techniques. What the media as
established will not permit, however, is a questioning of the
assumption that there is a population problem. Buckminster
Fuller's contention that the entire population of the world
and its projected increase could be handled with the
anticipatory design science of learning to do more with
less is a gospel embraced by only a small group of disciples.
This position violates the totalitarian questions of TV, to
say nothing of the entrenched fundamental theology of
commercial advertising.

A second telepolitical assumption is the conviction that
education is always a good thing and that the problems of
the world tend to wither away in proportion to the rise
of educational opportunities and equality. Dr. Ivan
Illich then crashes onto the scene and states just the
contrary: what the world needs is less and not more
education; more specifically, what South America is
suffering from is precisely too much education; let us,
then, "de-school society." His daringly radical proposals
have gained a hearing because of their novelty and his own
charismatic personality. The success of Illich is proportionate to his being misunderstood.

The day when he is understood will be the day when he is
relegated to the underground. His educational philosophy
simply is a heresy that cannot be reconciled with an
orthodoxy inherited from older generations who believe
that all problems can be solved by bigger and better
education. To come out, publicly and formally, on
television, against education is a declaration of insanity
or depravity. Even though the form of television renders

65

the older book culture obsolete, the content of television sets itself squarely against the genius of the medium itself.

Illich, we are told, was treated roughly by Vatican officials when he was called to Rome to give an account of his teachings at Cuernavaca. The accounting which will be demanded of him by an Establishment-dominated television, once television is cognizant of his game, will render his earlier encounter with an Inquisition pale by comparison. Illich will no longer be seen or talked about. He will become a non-person to the new electronic world. We give him another several years of delphic educational heresy before he is buried in silence or before he buckles under to Anglo-Saxon convictions about the highmindedness and importance of formal education centered around book learning, grades, and tests.

In the village, or at least in the village society, education is suspect. Making education available in the village can only make things worse. Consider Caliban in the tempest: the only good education has done him is that it taught him to curse. In Hardy's *Return of the Native*, the comments of the Captain on education proclaim that education leads to shamelessness and graffiti and nothing else. The village held education suspect because (1) it upset the ritual of life, and (2) it interfered with the learning process.

Let us contrast this with the city. In the city, there is no real ritual of life. *   Hence education need not worry about disrupting what does not exist. Further, because of the different labor situation, the learning process must be institutionalized. Therefore, there exists education as a formal structure. Perhaps it is only in the city that education has ever gained any sort of respectability. And the city has even canonized the process: very unvillage-like.

* Illich, Ivan, *De-Schooling Society,*(Harper and Row; New York 1971)

66

In short, formalized education is a creation of the city;
and a specific city, at that, the nineteenth century industrial
city. If only the educational establishment were honest enough
it would see the direct relationship between its existence
and the growth of sweatshop industry.

So --what happens when the city ceases to be and is replaced
by the global village? The educational system returns
naturally to its position as village nuisance. What we are
witnessing today in the schools across the continent is
the decomposition of a dead body. But you cannot ask
such questions on TV.

The collosal irony is missed by everybody. The electronic
form has effectively destroyed the city and has effectively
reduced formal education to a global nuisance. But the
masters of television act as though nothing new has
happened and drone on and on about saving the city and
improving education. Saving the city and improving
education are certainly the most totalitarian of all the
totalitarian questions.

10 Novelty as History

The dominant political attitude toward the electronic invasion
is more conservative than reactionary. The term "conservative"
does not refer to substantive issues associated with political
conservatism today. Both liberals and conservatives in the
common sense of the term are found to share the position
which we are calling "conservative" within the structure of
communications theory.

This attitude is not hostile to the new media. Pressure
groups and parties struggling for political power have
welcomed both television and the computer as new
instruments in the permanent game of politics. "Conservatism"
in media theory means that no ontologicial difference distin-
guishes new modes of communication from older ones. The

conservative is the progressivist. He holds that man progressed from print to telegraph to radio to television.

The underlying philosophy of progressivist conservatism is inherited from the eighteenth and nineteenth centuries. It holds that the historical advance of technology is linear. There is a direct line leading back from the computer to the symbolic structure of the alphabet.

No breaks are admitted in this linear history. One generation logically grows out of its predecessor and naturally prepares the way for its successor. Historical progressivism or conservatism is profoundly anti-revolutionary. No abrupt endings and beginnings are permitted in the story of man. History simply unpacks or develops what was already implicitly there in the past. The movement from horse and buggy to automobile was organic; from sailing ship to steamboat, organic; from print technology to television, organic.

It takes but a moment's reflection to see that any sophisticated theory of communications must reject progressivist conservatism.

The difference between horse and horseless carriage is absolute. Horses do not develop into engines. The difference between sail and steamboat is absolute; sails never turn into pistons. Organic links are found in needs; more speed is needed to cross ocean or prairie. But you can analyze the meaning of a horse from now to eternity and never come up with a Tin Lizzie. Finally, the difference between printed newspaper and televised newscast is just as absolute.

The newspaper is not a chrysalis developing into the butterfly of television. Content can be organic, but in the issue in question, the media represent an abrupt ending and a new beginning. The difference is not one of growth of expanding intelligibility, but of an otherness in orders of being. Historical changes, while admitting of the progressivist principle, are often as abrupt and unconnected as those exemplified in the horse and automobile. Einstein's world-shattering theory, $E = mc^2$, had nothing to do with Newtonian physics. His equation was absolutely new. The historical residue in most significant breakthroughs in physics is at best residual.

The continuum here is not in the new discovery but in the scientist who makes it. But man's visual bias as well as his interior awareness of a continuum in his own life demands that he discover continuity in history even where none exists. We do not deplore this passion for continuity. The continuum is man himself. But there is no continuum in the eruption of novelty in history.

11 The Death of Nationalism

A commonplace states that nationalism was the effect of a new print technology in the early modern age. This same technology both centralized political power, thus drying up older autonomous institutions, and simultaneously created a series of cerebralized ideas which summed up the intrinsic meaning of the national state. Liberty, Equality, Fraternity, Democracy, Progress, Science, National Sovereignty --none of these ideals can be "imaged" concretely. These are "abstract meanings," not "concrete beings," and the electronic image, no matter how unreal it might be, is nonetheless concretely being. The image is concrete in its own order of existence.

Nationalism was an external spatial expansion by one great power after another and wars in the age of nationalism were the result of spatial collisions between colossi on the march. But the spatial expansion was itself the consequence of an inner revolution of consciousness, Kant's famous *Second Copernican Revolution.* The cosmos or world of Kant was precisely that of Newtonian physics: space is "out there" before our eyes, infinite, beckoning us to cross the most distant horizon. Space was an absolute, that

69

absolute which appeared beyond the horizon to any
merchant adventurer setting his sails westward into the
Atlantic. No longer the iconic space of Medieval Man which
consisted of "intervals," Newtonian --modern-- space sent
explorers around the world and produced colonialism.
Given that space was an infinite "out there," man was not
constricted to where he was, nor was he confined to a
space understood in terms of a fence that creates a world
whose limits turn in upon their center, the cottage or house.
Space was the cowboy space; it was Horace Greeley's
"Go West, young man." Space was the liberty that beckoned
man to go from where he now was with all its constrictions.
The invention of barbed wire prefigured the Heisenberg
principle.

Now the conditions for this linear space are rooted,
according to the rationalist and idealist traditions in the
human consciousness as *a priori* principles through which
reason organizes the world of things. It follows that the
movement into space outwards was a movement in which
consciousness discovered itself in the concrete. This
doctrine, good German idealism, was actually a further
development of French rationalism's insistence that
consciousness is somehow prior to existence and that consciousness somehow orchestrates the whole order of being.
Meaning engenders reality. Ideas make history. History
does not make ideas. The crowning glory of Marx was to
have seen the fallacy of this consequent.

In nationalism, that very French creation, the meaning of
the French nation sets the Revolution to marching through
Europe and to extending the frontiers, those spatial and
Newtonian limits of its political sovereignty. Horace
Greeley's command to go West was a command to extend
the *meaning* of America into a geographical space moving
from east to west. Thus the modern national state
extended itself physically because it had discovered its own
spiritual meaning, its "Manifest Destiny."

The American military failure in Vietnam is largely predicated on the Pentagon's old-fashioned conviction that wars are won when spaces are occupied. This assumption of rationalist politics was first successfully challenged when Napoleon failed to conquer Spain even though his troops occupied the entire country. World War I's battle of the trenches on the western front was the last great rationalized war in history. Daily success or failure at Verdun was often mentioned in terms of yards occupied or lost.

The failure of France in World War II was the Maginot Line which was based on the assumption that military spaces correspond to old-fashioned political boundaries. The invention of the panzer corps exploded this eighteenth century conception. Spaces are mopped up after victory has essentially been achieved. But victory has nothing essentially to do with occupying spaces. The importance of tyranizing geographical space --i.e., German and Japanese raiders and submarines occupying vast spaces of the Pacific and the Atlantic-- was obliterated by radar.

Yet the American military complex at the time of the Vietnam war found itself ready to fight World War III on old spatial grounds, as generals have always been masters of the wars that went before.

Political analysts around the globe puzzle that the little man, the half-starved illiterate Viet Cong guerrilla has stupified and halted the most powerful military industrial complex in history. He has done no such thing. America has "lost" the first war in her history because of the very perfection of her electronic technology. This technology would not permit an "over there" war, but daily projected it --even as entertainment-- over here. *The Vietnam war is the first American foreign war to be fought on American soil.*

Within a non-Newtonian electronic world there is no possibility of any expansion outwards into Newtonian space. This kind of "space" is not annihilated but is abosrbed within a new order of being. Ex-plosion "outwards" yields to "im-plosion." The being of the imaged world implodes in man and this implosion is not spatial at all nor does it involve any necessary spatial concretization. Territorial expansion is absurd in a world that has already abolished space as an independent dimension of its own cosmos. Political action thus becomes an increasing intensity of identification by those who participate in the image.

The "cold" war has been a good example of an early war of images and identification. For twenty years and more the Soviet Union and the United States fought one another through the image of the enemy and of itself that it con- structed and projected around the world.

Using information to build an icon of the other, the war reached sublime coldness with the advent of even limited global television. Under electronic glare, for the first time in history, men could see both sides of a war at once. This is what the peace demonstrations were really about.

The image is profoundly personal in that we as persons, i.e., individuals, identify with the image. Knowledge is the identity of the knower and the thing known. The profoundly *personal* nature of the image went to war with the profoundly *impersonal* nature of ideologies. "Body count" became an intolerable contradiction in such a war. ("Body count" still survives in tribal warfare --the war in Ireland, for example-- because tribal warfare is personal.) Neuronic initiation into the being of the image takes the place of nationalist expansion and ideological warfare.

Nationalism moves not *inwards* into the consciousness but *outwards* from the consciousness. It moves towards an even higher centralized internationalism which is only an abstraction distilled from earlier abstractions that clustered around nationalism itself. The abolition of provincial cultures followed in the wake of the creation of the national state. Abstract with reference to local culture, the national state was concrete with reference to the internationalist ideal. Extending the abstraction and distilling still further the local springs of community, the internationalist ideal probably reached its apotheosis in people like Wendell Wilkie who confessed that he looked forward to the day when everyone would speak only one language and read one literature.

The re-birth of separatism today has been badly interpreted even by its own adherents who speak of the "nationalism" in Quebec, Scotland , Wales and Brittany. True nationalism reveres geography because space is understood to be a metaphysical absolute; the more real estate, the more prestigious the state. Nationalism is highly *impersonal.*

Tribal reverence for an enclosed space is personal: *our* fathers lived *here,* therefore this space is sacred. It is significant that the re-birth of nationalisms are always associated with small areas. They are sacred as was a Roman "grove," because it is the dwelling place of a god. Old tribal identification is highly personal.

12 Neuronic Absentmindedness

Neuronic identification is equally as personal, but increasingly the "space" within which this identification "takes place" is invented as a moment of time within a total process. Neuronic Man creates his own space. The hippie pad is as neuronic as is a 747 jet. Artifacted by intervals of time, these "spaces" cease to have any instrinsic or sacral meaning. Neuronic Man is uninterested in *things* organized in Newtonian space. His non-materialism is one with his wishing not to be burdened as he moves on. A pile of household goods is simply an added expense and a nuisance to carry around. Since Neuronic Man literally cannot *see* because his visuality is dissolved in tactility, the visual contemplation

of a filled space leaves him cold. He cannot understand his
elderly aunts fussing over the hardware of furniture.

Neuronic man bifurcates into reactionary and post-modern.
The older tribes, revived by telepolitical imagery, fiercely
return to their ancient groves but the new tribes carry
their groves in jean pockets as they jet around the globe
or hitchhike from town to town. In both cases geography
as mere real estate ceases to be a significant dimension of
the human psyche.

The end result is the increasing "de-geographisization" of
politics. The nearest historical parallel to this phenomenon
in the West is late medieval and early modern Burgundy.
Just as the national state was created and became the new
form of society, the Middle Ages returned as *content* with
Burgundy. Chivalry; trans-national Christendom; the
crusading spirit: all of these swarmed into the Burgundian
consciousness precisely when they had ceased being the
dominant political ground in Europe. Burgundy never had
a geographical center. The boundaries of the duchy not
only changed; the very center of the duchy shifted. At
one point Burgundy's geography so totally changed that
where it was yesterday was precisely where it was not the
day after. Burgundy was the Order of the Golden Fleece,
medieval content reposing on a new commercial ground.
Burgundy was a state of mind.

Neuronic Man today is the new form of which Burgundy
was the old content. Rootless, he adores roots. Electronic,
he spends his spare time tinkering with old cars.

We offer a tip to the reader: suppress the content of what
Neuronic Man says. Watch what he does! What he does is
often in contradiction to what he says. The fiercest of
American patriots are the ex-patriots living in Guadalajara
and Acapulco in Mexico. Mexico pullulates with retired
military personnel who kiss the American soil --from

Mexico. Space, as an independent reality, has ceased to be taken seriously in an electronic world within which space is a domesticated nuisance. Neuronicism is global gypsyism as form. As content neuronicism is McLuhan's understanding of the past as an artform. You can be neuronic by putting on the audience of any and every historical epoch. History is the wardrobe of the present.

As a ground or gestalt of a new civilization, as a man having a "bias of communication," as Harold Innis would have put it, Neuronic Man is largely innocent of who he is or of what he is up to. More precisely: as indicated, he is always "up to and about" exactly that which he says he is not. Interpreting himself in terms of an immediate or --more rarely-- remote past, Neuronic Man is totally formed by electronic circuitry. Yet he is absolutely naive about the new world into which he has been catapulted.

Part III
Neuronic Wars

1 Monstration by Television: The Spanish Case

Recently a retired French general made a study of the relationship between war and television. He was invited by the
Spanish Ministry of Information and Tourism to lecture
on his conclusions. Before the assembled group of
ministers and bureaucrats the general discussed the theory
of taking over a nation by way of infiltrating and seizing
the power of electronic media. Differing from older
psychological warfare, this new strategy suggested a warfare from within which would subtly and non-violently
change a national psychology. The general illustrated his
thesis with copious quotations from psychological literature
and visually with elaborately-constructed charts. At the end
of his discourse he was applauded roundly by the Spanish
civil servants and duly congratulated for the lucidity and
brilliance of his discourse. The lecturer went home and so
did his audience, never dreaming he had been talking
about Spain!

Despite an astonishing stream of tourists, forging into the
millions, Spain has remained a mystery to western Europe
and to the United States. The mystery was deepened by
mutual bitterness immediately after World War II when the
United Nations, in an effort to unseat the Franco regime,
blockaded Spain. This overt act of hostility united a nation

which had been bitterly divided by the Civil War of 1936-
39. Instead of rejecting the Franco victory, an economically-
devastated nation rallied behind him and defied the outside
world. This act of defiance which took hunger and poverty
in good cheer in the name of Spanish independence from
outside pressure has deteriorated since the introduction
of television into the country.

The ancient physical barrier of the Pyrenees --where
Europe ends and Africa begins, according to the philosopher,
Unamuno-- has tended to isolate Spain from the rest of
Europe throughout history. The deep interior mountain
divisions have isolated one region from another and produced deep provincial distinctions and sub-cultures. This
isolationism has been shattered by the form of television
which destroys boundaries. The Pyrenees do not exist
for electronic information movement.

The content of Spanish television is largely imported.
Dominated by western modes of thinking and styles of
being, Spanish TV has slowly changed the national psyche.
Spanish youngsters have been bred on *Rifleman* and
Bonanza. They have been exposed to the puritan work
ethic. A nation traditionally impatient with the orderly
processes of law has learned that the cowboy hero prevents the mob from lynching the gunman as he shields
the bad man until the circuit judge rides into town and
arranges for an orderly trial. The entire mythology woven
into the world of western television has little or nothing to
do with the Spanish historical experience. Female broadcasters, huckstering commercial products, wear French and
American fashions. Often they reflect the excessive blond
slenderness of the Vogue model which is not paradigmatic
of Spanish concepts of feminine beauty. More significantly,
commercial television inserts a consumer mentality into a
people that hitherto has taken an aesthetic pride in being
ascetic.

Don Quixote and Sancho Panza symbolize the Spanish spirit.
This quixotic juxtaposition of romantic and chivalric dedication pushed to the razor's edge of sanity, linked with the
gross materialism of Sancho, has worked its paradox into
the Spanish spirit. Admitting that the pursuit of *things* is
one with human nature, Spain --thanks to a stoicism, already
present in Seneca, later united with a lyrical commitment
to Catholic Christianity-- accepted the fact of materialism
but refused to admire it. Everybody wants to have it
better than he has, but this truth is not to be adored; it
is to be mocked.

Commercial television, on the contrary, insists that consumption be taken with deadly seriousness. The products that
flash over the screen are presented as solutions to the problems of life; they are threats against men remaining as they
are. They disturb the classical Spanish indolence. The new
consumer mentality, reflected in a burgeoning economy in
the Spain of today, is transforming the psyche of the
nation, most especially of the young. The brilliant cartoons
of Mingote in Madrid's daily, the *ABC,* often highlight the
contrast. The Latin love of things --beautiful women and
much land in the past, now cars and refrigerators, comfort
and luxury, but luxury more than comfort-- accepted with
a cynical shrug by older generations annealed in the severity
of an essentially poor country, has become a religion with
the young. Television, the medium, is the cause.

The telepolitical revolution finds in Spain a uniquely interesting case. The Nationalist victory in 1939 closed the
bloodiest civil war of the century fought within the western
world. The mythology hammered out of three years of
fighting centered around "The 18th of July," 1936, when
traditionalist Spain rose in rebellion against the radical anti-
clerical Republic. The Franco victory delivered the entire
system of education into the hands of the new government.
Every child took, and takes, a course in the ideals of "The
National Movement." Every child went, and goes, to
summer camps run by the official government party, the

Falange. Mass demonstrations reiterated the goals of
victory. The official hymn, "Face to the Sun"; the
Falangist salute under a Castillian sky reflected the political
romanticism of Ortega y Gasset, the intellectual mentor
of the Falange's founder, José Antonio Primo de Rivera;
the new identity of Church and People; the promised
transcendence of the old class war; the conviction that a
million men had died --not for economics but for the things
of the spirit-- infused the heart of victorious Nationalist,
Catholic Spain.

None of this obliterated Sancho Panza. A famous joke of
the late forties and fifties had elephant watchers writing
books as follows: The American Elephant -- bigger and
better; the British Elephant --product of the Empire; the
German Elephant --known sketchily through a five-volume
introduction to his habitat and being; the French Elephant
-- and his love life; the Spanish Elephant --the carrier of
Eternal Values. An older order may have won the
revolution but Don Quixote continued to exist side by
side with Sancho Panza. It was all very Spanish.

The defeated were cowed and silent and even hid their
participation in, or sympathy for, the old Communist
Republic. The labor unions were run by the official
Falange. The press was rigidly controlled. But it did not
last. By the late 1950's, the steam had gone out of the
Nationalist Movement; youth was looking elsewhere.

The more than one and a half million veterans who had been
enthusiastic volunteers in the Nationalist cause, now viewed
in dismay the hostile reaction of their sons. Why did
Nationalist Spain fail to work its mythology into the
substance of the young, as the victorious North American
Union had done in the years that followed the Civil War
between the States?

Although it would be a simplification to reduce the nexus of
causality to the failure to exploit the new medium of tele-

80

vision, that failure is certainly a principle cause of Spain's drift towards radicalization today. The Franco regime never took television seriously. Those thinkers who were interested in exploring the new medium --Marias and Aranguren, for example-- were men of the political left. The broadcasters and technicians and programmers who moved into television largely were men out of sympathy with the regime. They could not openly *demonstrate* their opposition. Therefore, they *monstrated* it by simply flashing another world into Spain's bars and homes, a world having little to do with the blue-shirted Falange, Holy Week processions in Seville, cathedrals of Burgos and Barcelona, austere villages on the parched plains of Castille. This outside world reflected democratic uniformity, affluence, a vision of the real directed toward an earth which was clever enough not to contradict Heaven, but simply to ignore it!

2 Television and the New Quebec

Just how quickly and cataclysmically television can change a society is evinced in modern Quebec.

Here was a society --usually described in old guide books as "quaint"-- whose cultural values and social patterns had remained basically unchanged for four centuries. It reposed upon an agricultural economy going back to pre-revolution-ary France that was aristocratic and feudal. Not even in the South of the United States was family structure so intimidating. The French settlers were uniformly Roman Catholic, with the Church both founding and controlling all educational institutions. A strong Jansenist streak further bound the society into rigid codes of behavior -- puritanism in some form seems to have been a necessity for survival for all early settlers of this continent. After the British conquest, Quebec remained shut off from the growing atheism and materialism of the rest of North America by language, customs and religion, the three guarantees made to French settlers in the Act of Quebec in

81

1774, and later confirmed by the British North America Act at the founding of Canada in 1867.

Feeling abandoned by the French --the most poignant ballad sung by French Canadians goes *J'ai perdu ma maîtresse Sans l'avoir mérité. Lui ya longtemps que je t'aime, Jamais, je ne t'oublierai.* --I lost my beloved (i.e., France) without having deserved to. For so long loved you. Never will I forget you.--" and humiliated by the English, Quebec nurtured in her isolation the conviction that God had ordained a special role for the French Quebecer to fill in history. The late historian Canon Lionel Groulx* was a major exponent of this thesis that the French in Quebec could not have suffered so much and survived so long for nothing.

Although World War II corroded the older agrarian society around the edges with industrialization, and the benevolent dictator Maurice Duplessis --Canada's Huey Long-- encouraged French Quebecers to go into business and self-consciously created French-Canadian millionaires, nevertheless as late as 1950, family, educational, religious and social attitudes remained much as they had always been.

The history of the new Quebec can be dated BTV and ATV --Before Television and After Television.

In the 1940's Quebec had the strictest film censorship in North America. Children under sixteen were not allowed into movie houses, even with parents --the only exception being an occasional Disney extravaganza. Every mention of the word "divorce" was cut out of films, sometimes causing havoc with the plot. Adulterous kissing was likewise deleted. The famous Paul Muni film of the life of Emile Zola was banned entirely. No book on the Index could be taken out of Montreal's public library without

*Histoire du Canada français depuis la découverte, 2 vols. (Montréal: Fides, 1969)

proof of scholarly disinterest; no bookstore offered Gide
or Proust for sale in the original French.

Everyone went to Mass. There was no civil marriage and
no legal divorce. The Government of Canada did provide
through the Senate, a form of expensive and lengthy divorce
for Quebec residents, but the Provincial courts were under no
obligation to recognize it. Outside of Montreal, it was
difficult to find a drugstore that sold contraceptives.

Evolution and Marxism and Freudianism, main winds that
had shaken Europe for a century, were not even breezes
rippling the surface of Quebec life. The society was pa-
triarchal. Little mobility was possible outside the Church,
the main artery for channeling the ambitions of the poor.
A hierarchical order clustered around priest, lawyer, doctor,
notary and farmer. Compulsory education was not made
law until 1943. In the elementary schools, learning was
largely by rote. Classical colleges run by the Church
emphasized Latin, Greek and seventeenth century French
dramatists and poets. Philosophy was central. Science
and commerce and engineering were peripheral subjects.
The end of higher education was the *formation* of the
student in the "forms" of reality, the structures in which
things were, should be, and must be. Without this formal
polish to his personality, even the brightest lad was nothing.
The code of medical practice was decided by religion, and
French-Canadian hospitals were widely staffed by nuns. A
woman in labor could not get access to such a hospital
unless accompanied, or vouched for, by her husband.
Unmarried mothers had their own hospitals.

In Montreal and, to a much lesser extent, in Quebec City,
the English minority went its own way, living within, but
cut off from, the French-speaking world surrounding it.
The English Quebecers were contemptuous of the supposed
"backwardness" of French Canadians, even as they used
them as workers. Bartering advantages from, and yielding
points to, the French political leaders and the Church, the

83

English retained their privileged status within the community, controlled its wealth and dominated its industry. Even when control of many major industries in Quebec passed from England to the United States, and American investment came to be a dominant fact and frustration of the Quebec economy --as, indeed, it became of all the Canadian economy;-- the English-speaking dominance did not change.

Even so, many French Quebecers who were born and grew up in the Quebec of the first half of this century considered it a very good place to live, where people were at inner peace with themselves and outer peace with the world, where every man knew who he was, what his place in the world was was, where he was going, what he could do and could not do.

Then came the revolution.

Quebecers date their revolution from everything *except* the advent of television. In that, they share the media misunderstanding that plagues the entire industrialized world. They locate their revolution in *content* rather than *form.*

Some artists and intellectuals date it from 1948 and the publication of Paul-Emile Borduas' *Refus Global*, an artists' manifesto that created an uproar for its attack on the traditional institutions and values of Quebec and brought about the dismissal of Borduas from his teaching post in the government-run graphic arts school, his exile first to New York City and finally to Paris where he died in 1960.

Sociologists and economists are fond of 1949 as "the date" when the famous Asbestos strike saw the maturing of the French-Canadian trade union movement, the first signs of Church support moving away from employers towards workers, and the debut of Trudeau as a lawyer for the strikers.

But Quebec has a long history of attempts to change it by individuals and small groups who rose to brief notoriety and lapsed into silence or exile. Would either of the above have ended differently if television had not come to Quebec so soon afterwards? We argue "no."

In September 1952 the Canadian Broadcasting Corporation opened its first TV station in Montreal, a bilingual one soon to be separate French and English networks. As if in response to a pre-arranged signal, antennas sprang from rooftops -even from country shacks so far from the broadcast area that only the faintest of pictures could be picked up. Surprisingly little of even early French-Canadian television was canned. Old French films and dubbed-in American sit-coms and shoot-em-ups were shown, but the proportion was less than one would expect. In this, the TV revolution in Quebec differs significantly from the TV revolution in Spain.

Overnight a new class of people was hurried into being-- the French-Canadian TV personality. This new elite has been the most important single factor in helping establish the mythos of the new Quebec. They simply monstrated electronically a new kind of French Canadian. Sophisticated, handsomely dressed, witty and worldly, these new TV people --the first of the "beautiful people"-- flashed an image utterly foreign to the aristocratic, prim, somewhat stuffy, image of the upper-class Quebecer of the past. It was even more remote from that picture of the French-Canadian worker as a good-natured, beer-drinking, rough and-tumble, *joual*-talking *habitant*, content with his family, his church and his traditional way of life.

French Canada had long possessed a group of stand-up comics far superior to anything English Canada could boast --the natural offshoot of an essentially oral society where the raconteur was the most precious of companions. These too now came into their own, as did the superb actors whose talents had hitherto been limited to radio and to the repertory theaters of Montreal. Although many of the talk shows and quiz shows in French paralleled standard U.S. shows, the subject matter was Quebec and its problems, and no idea or opinion seemed too *osé*, too outrageous or too intimate, for open discussion.

Women swarmed into prominence. Where only a few years before any girl who entered professional studies at the university had to brave a barrage of ridicule that cast doubts on her ability to "make it" as a female (i.e., get a man) and where the right and proper education for upper-class young ladies was the right convent finishing school, suddenly women emerged as the intellectual equals of men, conducting their own shows,arguing from very liberated stances, and generally projecting an image that had little to do with the *Kinder, Kirche, Küche* role to which the average French Quebec woman had been limited.

By the time the Quebec Government came up with the confidence-encouraging slogan *Québec sait faire,* it was no longer needed. Every Quebecer who watched TV believed in his heart that Quebec knew how!

This "knowing how" is one with the new TV style. TV personalities in Quebec at this writing are treated like Hollywood stars in the thirties. Nearly a dozen weekly tabloids recount their antics and publish their *"secrets,"* *(Tele-Radiomonde, Journal des Vedettes, Secrets des Vedettes, Echos-Vedettes, etc.)*Posters flash their faces everywhere. Singers, comedians, actors,interviewers, reporters-turned-commentators --all form a new estate in Quebec. And most viewers get the message: the new elite is largely separatist.

Many rode, triumphantly waving to their cheering fans, from their seats atop the rolled-down hoods of convertibles in St-Jean Baptiste parades through the 1960's as these became, ever more violently, separatist demonstrations.

They were arrested in protest marches, picked up during the War Measures Act. Even when they did not openly declare for separatism, their sympathies were imaged, monstrated to the public.

Everyone understood. To share vicariously in the life of this exciting and beautiful people of the new Quebec was to be for an independent Quebec.

While the United States has a number of movie stars who have been transmogrified into politicians in the neuronic age, so far as we are aware Quebec has the first TV personality to become a political leader. For René Lévesque to move from news commentator to the leadership of the separatist Parti Québecois is almost the equivalent of an Eric Sevareid or a Howard K. Smith heading a new --and secessionist-- third party in the United States. Almost, but not quite. For René Lévesque's TV style was unique.

He had been a newspaperman. On TV he became a news analyst commenting on the late evening news. One Quebecer who remembers those programs from the fifties gave us the following description:

"It was a cliff-hanger style. He was not cool or quiet or reasonable, like the leading U.S. analysts. He was positively passionate, waving his arms about, his thin, ascetic face reflecting the intensity of the news. If you didn't understand French you might have thought he was exhorting you to repent your sins, that the end of the world was at hand. He talked with a desperate urgency, with maps and blackboards as props, as if in a life-death struggle to make you *understand.* His 'that's the way it is' trademark at the end was a sudden unexpected smile and shrug, that could convey anything from pity, to irony, to satisfaction."

To the average Quebecer whose knowledge of the world came from where the Quebec Church had its missionaries stationed, Lévesque was a window outwards. Through

87

those years so many new national states were establishing themselves, the question could not escape the viewer: *"Pourquoi pas nous, aussi?"* Nor was it surprising that when the time came to choose a man to unite all the factions that wanted a separate Quebec, Lévesque was turned to. Anyone who knew so much about the world ought to know how to lead his people into a new world.

By the time the Parti Québecois came into being, Lévesque had already won his spurs *--gagné ses épaulettes--* politically. He first showed leadership during a strike of CBC producers in 1959. From there he went into the provincial Liberal Party, became a cabinet minister and brought about the nationalization of Quebec's hydro-electric companies,and finally split from the Establishment to lead the united separatist party.

The Parti Québecois is a creature of the TV screen: sufficiently blurred, it invites the viewer to read into it whatever he wants, to imagine in that future independent Quebec whatever utopia he wishes. The Parti Québecois can thus combine an impressive range of political ideologies. Like an umbrella it covers Maoist terrorist groups, with Cuban, North-African or Arab connections, as well as the *petite bourgeoisie* of the old traditionalist St-Jean Baptiste Society. All are held together in a tenuous web by the central objective of independence *now.*

Lévesque remains an interesting figure telepolitically. An obsessive and nervous smoker, he never seems in repose. His body as well as his face are mobile and restless. In this he seems to sum up the electronic impatience with time that can be sensed everywhere in Quebec. Independence must come *now* --or at least in the next election-- or all this energy and drive and devotion may somehow dissipate itself.

Older Quebecers who have lived through the last decade are still trying to recover from the cultural shock of that experience. In 1960, following the death of Duplessis the preceding fall, the "quiet revolution" that had been building up through the last years of the 1950's emerged simultaneously on several levels. At first it seemed more like a reform movement than a revolution, as the newly-elected provincial Liberal Party put through vast changes in education and social welfare. By 1970, however, the "quiet" was gone. Terrorist bombs exploded; police were confronted in parades, marches, protests and riots; universities --but recently expanded to take in everyone who could pass the entrance requirements-- were shut down with sit-ins; until finally, in the fall of 1970, political kidnappings and political murder put Quebec on the front pages and projected it across the TV screens of the world.

It was quite a decade.

Everything old Quebecers were brought up to consider forbidden and undesirable, everything they had brought up their own children to so consider, was offered and advocated on all sides. Where once Quebec had the strict-est censorship in North America, it now had the most le-nient. Bookstores burgeoned and sold everything, as long as it was in French. Some Quebec newsstands looked like the pornographic bookshops around 42nd and Broadway.

Movies shown on Quebec French TV today reveal more skin than any shown on U.S. stations. Sex information, still mostly confined to books and magazines in the U.S., is offered as casually in Quebec French newspapers as our *Dear Abby.* Quebec now has its own divorce courts and civil weddings. Contraceptive information and abortion are advertised. While nudism on stage is not particularly unusual these days in the United States, a group of young school teachers in Montreal provided a new dimension in what they called a "theater of terrorism." Not only did they appear on the stage of the Comédie Canadienne nude, but they then proceeded to slaughter a live fowl and smear their bodies with its blood. Quebec can also claim the distinction of having the most celebrated public "wedding" of two homosexuals to take place thus far in North America.

Meanwhile in the Vatican old churchmen shake their heads. The Roman Catholic Church in Quebec which only a few years ago could be counted upon to vote with the Spanish and South American Churches as the most conservative in the Catholic world was now even pushier than the U.S. Church for the "liberalizing" of Church rules.

The audial basis of television has been nowhere more striking than in Quebec. In old Quebec everyday French was not very good French. Children in their new drive for education and their confrontations in the name of making French not only the official and working language of Quebec, but the *only* language of Quebec, were ashamed of their parents' inability to talk the language well. The contrast between the language spoken in the kitchen and the language spoken in the living room by those beautiful TV people could escape no one. To speak French correctly became an obsession. To do so, it was necessary to get rid of *joual,* the patois of Quebec that combined old French with bad grammar, American slang, franglais and English sentence structures in accents that made it unintelligible to the non-Quebecer. The new educators attacked the problem with dedication. Discussions about correct French sometimes took as much space as politics on editorial pages. But abhorent as *joual* was and virulent as the efforts were to get rid of it, it declined as speech to emerge as art! Today the most brilliant of Quebec's new playwrights, Michel Tremblay, and the brightest of its new comedians, Yvon Deschamps, use *joual* as a kind of tragi-comic medium, full of humor, earthiness, poignancy and dramatic power --much as their Jewish counterparts in the U.S. have used Yiddish. That their performances and plays are sold out almost as soon as announced suggests that Quebec --for all its self-conscious drive to purify its

French-- still regards with deep affection the Quebec that once was.

In that old Quebec separateness was nourished as a means of living a good life here and assuring eternal life hereafter. The new separatism now returns as myth based on language alone.

Will Quebec separate from Canada?   Will the Quebec revolution end with a new national state being established on the banks of the St. Lawrence?

While on the one hand the Parti Québecois seems to grow steadily in size and René Lévesque seems to grow more conservative as he gets closer to the reins of power, there are also signs of the fragmentization taking place that we believe to be the immediate future of telepolitical societies. What happened in May, 1972 as the three trade union movements of Quebec formed a *front commun* and tried to lead a general strike against the Quebec Government is an example of this. It was a lively two weeks with commando-types taking over radio stations for a few hours, closing down all Montreal newspapers for a day, forcing shops in Sherbrooke to close for a morning, shutting down the whole town of Sept-Iles for several days, even forcing the main separatist weekly *Québec Presse* to leave out the column of their distinguished economist Jacques Parizeau because he had not taken the proper attitude toward the common front.

But the unions were not able to arouse united loyalty, even with union leaders in jail as martyrs who had refused to appeal contempt of court charges. Instead of the general support expected, secessionist movements broke out in the unions themselves, and the leaders came out of jail to find a new, and fourth, major trade union movement sprung full-grown as it were from the confusion. Telepolitical man may be easily aroused to action, but his attention-span is short. Perhaps he is impatient pre-

91

cisely because perseverence in long-range and widely-based
general objectives is so hard for him.

Because Quebec presents such a speeded-up picture of telepolitical man, it is a key place to watch in the years
immediately ahead of us.

3 Televised Kidnapping

In the past nothing could have been more private than a
kidnapping. It was of the essence of the act that the kid-
nappers remain shrouded in anonymity, that the extortionist
notes be kept from the knowledge of the police, that the
whereabouts of the victim never be revealed.

Such was --and remains-- kidnapping, outside the new order
of Telepolitics.

The British diplomat Richard Cross --tucked away in the
back room of a north-end Montreal flat-- watched over
television the funeral of Quebec labor minister Pierre Laporte,
kidnapped after him and killed by his abductors.

Nobody knows at this writing whether the Berrigan brothers
and their colleagues in that famous conversation were serious
or only speculating abstractly over drinks. In any event,
their plan as reported involved kidnapping a national figure,
perhaps Kissinger, and then filming him as he was being
interrogated by his captors. The kidnapping was, of course,
to be a secret act *outside* the media in the "real" world, but
the secrecy was to be abolished *within* the media. Anyone
with an itch for paradox must, at least, sense that something
new has entered into human existence. What is private and
what is public anymore in a telepolitical world?

Kidnapping, in common with murder, must be done privately.
Who wants to get caught or found out? Before answering
"No one," we must reflect on the nature of political

92

murder or its attempts in recent years. Robert Kennedy was murdered publicly in a Los Angeles hotel. Jack Ruby murdered Lee Harvey Oswald before a television audience of several million. George Wallace was shot in a shopping center while TV cameras turned. The Pope in the Philippines was daggered at by a Bolivian artist before a live audience of thousands and a television audience of millions.

The question is not resolved by suggesting these killers were deranged. The magic of a telepolical world bewitches escape from deranged privaçy through entrance into telepolitical enchantment --with a dagger or a pistol. The case histories of Ruby and Sirhan Sirhan point towards frustrated lives released in one glorious moment in which existence is transmogrified into theater. That it is macabre theater ought to make us look even more carefully at what is truly a new reality.

4 Demonstrations and the Numbers Racket

The politics of demonstrations is a further case in point.

The new media heat up the potential violence in our environment by beaming problems into everyone's room, everywhere. The abolition of space and time in the telepolitical universe rendered it possible for the hippie life style to leap fully developed into history all over the planet --simultaneously and without any planning from some center of power.

The tactic of the demonstration was largely futile against the modern technologized state until the last decade. Demonstrations either failed or developed into bloody street wars, and these wars had always been won by the power of the gun. We need only think of 1956-1957: Budapest, Warsaw, East Berlin. By televising the demonstrations in the western world, the message is flashed to the whole globe and marching thousands are converted into marching

93

millions that threaten the Establishment everywhere in the West.

Bloody repression is tempered, as in Prague in 1968. Prague, and the events that followed the abortive show of independence by the Czechs, was Budapest, slowed down. The Russians could not act with their old savage speed. This tactic would have been too hot for the watching world and hence it would have been bad politics. The revenge had to be strung out over months of cooling off in which the attention of the world was gradually shifted to other issues and places.

Numbers lose their importance. The hard-hat demonstrations in New York in support of President Nixon's Vietnam policy were made to look simultaneously sinister, silly, and small. Anti-Vietnam demonstrations have been, through total coverage, made to look like the conscience of an outraged nation. When the masters of media are in sympathy with demonstrations they can turn a small show of force on the streets into massive proportions. When the media are out of sympathy with the demonstrators they can minimize and even totally destroy the effectiveness of the largest demonstrations.

5 Politics as Politics no Longer Exists

Naivete about the effects of electronic technology on the social and political order is traceable partially to the reduction of politics to content and to a subsequent loss of form. Any reasonably-educated non-specialist in medieval history has a fairly accurate understanding of the form of the medieval social order, structured --as it were-- into dynastic kingdoms, chartered towns, independent guilds; feudal nobility and serfdom; religious orders; Emperor and Pope. But that same reasonably-educated man most probably would be at a loss if questioned about the specific content of this or that historical event within the period. For his purposes, an understanding of medieval forms suffices for an intelligent insight into the structure of medieval society.

A similar instance could be drawn from the structure of the Roman Republic. The plebians were represented by the comitia; the aristocracy by the senate; the executive was in the hands of the consuls. A relatively simple and basic fundamental law inherited from the "Fathers" was interpreted by the judges. A basically juridical, legal, and non-philosophical society was structured around a sense of *pietas,* piety towards the past which invested its leaders with a style of life summed up by *gravitas,* solemnity, dignity, and measured decorum. Understanding this nexus of social forms, an educated man has sufficient information to form a reasonably accurate judgment about the structure of republican, aristocratic, Roman society.

From the Age of Enlightenment until today, however, this formal epistemology has been obscured. We have been taught to think of politics as being constituted by political content --programs, party platforms, ideological commitments. The remote cause of this change is the Cartesian shift in emphasis from "being" to "meaning," from reality to the interior of consciousness. When the political order ceased to be an exercise in being, a play, when it became a series of social programs to be achieved by way of deductions from a series of political "ideas" --i.e., "The Rights of Man,"-- emphasis moved largely from political forms to political content.

In America the primacy of content was simultaneously buttressed by the seriousness imposed by the puritan ethic. The intense man always has his eye on ends. Existential factors are seen by him as conditions to be altered in the service of his goals rather than as forms of being in which a community enshrines a way of life. This fixity of attention upon goals prevents men from looking at forms themselves as causes of being. But this hypnotic trance does not prevent men being transformed by media absent-mindedly. It even makes the transformation easier!

The concentration by critics on the content of television has atrophied their capacity to see television as a new form. Televised content --excepting the news-- is largely a-political. Therefore, so runs the conclusion, television is not a significant political factor.

Marshall McLuhan has written, "media produce a mass of effects in psyche and society." An hypnotic preoccupation with content obscures the fact that the new TV form is radically political in itself. Furthermore, the effect is achieved subconsciously, without the viewer being aware of analyzing or making a choice or often even "remembering." Eric Sevareid complained wryly at the close of his news commentary one evening that nobody remembers the next morning what a commentator said the night before. Inveterate TV watchers rarely remember the next morning the late movie of the night before. Some have trouble even remembering its title, to say nothing of its specific plot.

Millions of men and women and children sit watching the tube hour after hour, being altered sensorially, letting its message --the form, the medium-- work itself into their very lives.

6 The Totalitarian Now

A curious ambiguity governs the attitude of the networks towards their role in society. They believe they are reporting news; in fact, they always *create* news. Hence, they produce a cluster of effects in the body politic that are thoroughly *political* in nature. Unaware consciously that they have become a partner in politics rather than a reporter of politics, the media are one-eyed Cyclops, innocent of their own power.

Illustrative of this formal change in politics is global impatience with existing problems. Perennial poverty must be abolished *right now!* Four hundred years of machine-produced pollution must be cured *right now!* Wars must be ended *right now!*

Demands made by politicans out of power cannot be met by politicians in power. Older revolutions were achieved by visionaries who projected their expectations into the future. We live today in an age of constant revolution. Every problem is acutely known to everybody and screams out for immediate solution.

Older political institutions and forms simply cannot deliver the goods. This sentiment is not a moral judgment: we are unaware of any political forms that could assuage the winter of discontent that sweeps our globe in these declining years of the century.

An age raised on print tended to project visually-imagined solutions. This print-oriented generation then moved towards its projected future. But an age raised on the instantaneity of television has lost the future as a significant dimension of life. This is the "Now Generation."

Few social critics and even fewer political organizations aiming at, or exercising, power have taken the trouble or have the ability to confront boldly and explore delicately the radical transformation of politics being effected within the catalyst of the electronic revolution.

Perhaps politics as politics no longer exists.

7 Technology and Ethics: South Africa

The most advanced Praetorian attitude toward media is reducible to a cynical utilitarianism which is well-expressed in the old German saying, *"Der Mohr hat sein Schuld getan; Der Mohr kann gehen.* --The Moor has done his duty; the

97

Moor can go! " Use media to gain power. Then suppress media in the name of *our* way of life!

The opposition to electronic media finds its apotheosis in the Union of South Africa. When astronaut Collins quipped from space that he was the only person not watching on television as his comrades romped over lunar surfaces, he was ignoring the prohibition by law of television in the Union of South Africa. The reasons for this prohibition are complex. (Amusingly enough, underdeveloped Black republics to the north watched the moon invasion whereas affluent South Africans to the south had to read about it in the press.) The advent of television would tip the balance in favor of English and against Boer. Television would beam a secularized world into the homes of a nation officially committed to the old puritan ethic of its ancestors; television would shake to its foundation the official policy of apartheid. The attitude of the nationalist government reflects the sundering sword of philosophy, governing man's relationship with his own technological environment.

The classical and Christian tradition always insisted that the technological order was a "pure" instrument which could be taken up or set aside at the judgment of its human creator. Theoretically, every canon of the older ethical tradition insists that only man has rights. Therefore, no technological possibility can lay claim to existence simply because it *is* a possibility. No ethician annealed in the older tradition can dispute the proposition. Art has no rights over man. Translated into political terms, this means that a society has the right, possibly even the duty, to do all that is necessary to conserve its style of life. If South Africa is convinced: (a) that its way of life is a good way of life, and (b) that television will destroy that way of life, the suppression of television becomes the only logical conclusion to a political syllogism.

The classical and Christian tradition concerning the subordination of technology to ethics can scarcely be questioned in the terms in which it was cast: e.g., a sculptor ought not to ruin his health and catch TB by sacrificing himself to his work in a Parisian attic; Rimbaud dropped poetry before he was twenty and took up gunrunning because he intuited dumbly that his explorations in sensation were destroying his humanity; Oppenheimer dropped nuclear physics and became a common trafficker in scientific secrets because he feared an atomic holocaust.

The trouble with the traditional reasoning is its excessive abstractionism on the one hand and its excessive personalism on the other. Abstractly, nobody can seriously doubt the proposition that switchblades ought not to dominate a civilized community, no matter how artfully they are used. But these abstract propositions can only be entertained seriously by individuals, by persons. Once a technology gets a foot into existence, it spreads throughout the entire culture and creates its own environment. If you live in the inner city where switchblades are the rule, you had better buy one and learn how to use it.

8 Power versus Ethics

The classical and Christian ethic or, for that matter, international world government could work only if all nations accepted the same rules of the game. When one society picks up a new invention, other societies must do the same in the name of self-preservation. This was true of Chinese gunpowder, the Prussian percussion rifle, English tank warfare, and American atomic bombs, and of every other technological advance capable of giving tactical superiority to the society possessing it. It follows that technological possibility thus far has always involved its historical actualization sooner or later. Power politics here opposes ethics.

Marshall McLuhan has said that if we really understood the effects of television, we would shut it off for five years until we were prepared to handle the consequences of the effects. Possibly this is why the Chinese did not use the compass for 1,000 years after they had invented it. Western Man in fact and in principle since Machiavelli has usually opted for power over ethical considerations. This can hardly be defended in categories proper to conventional morality. But such loyalty is there, nonetheless. It exists. Meaning in tribal life is one with action. This action is always symbolic especially if the symbol be the gesture of laying down one's life for one's own.

9 Northern Ireland

Our major commentators today are bewildered and vaguely guilty about the civil war in Northern Ireland because they cannot come to grips with a tribal war that has erupted all over the world, thanks to electronic simultaneity. Howard K. Smith, the distinguished ABC news commentator, suggested that the drift into bloody civil war in Ireland is so grave that it needs a moderator. His candidate: Earl Warren. A judge! While, in theory, it is possible that a judge could measure the rights and wrongs of the Protestant Ulstermen against the Catholic minority in Northern Ireland and come up with a verdict, there would be no point in making the effort. For what Mr. Smith does not know is the brutal, even savage, truth that neither Catholic nor Protestant Ireland wants a judge because *both* know "the truth"about Ireland. That "truth" is not some past to be scrutinized objectively in court in order that its main lineaments be made clear. That "truth" or, more precisely, those two "truths" are two mythologies within which two people live and without which each would die.

The mythologies are supremely telepolitical and they disturb men in religion who make a profession out of ecumenism. Northern Ireland and its war chased Vietnam off American television in the declining months of 1971 and the opening months of 1972. Everybody was bored with those "gooks" nobody could see and those helicopters

that never seemed to go anywhere. But nobody was
bored with Bloody Sunday: the thirteen coffins carrying
the bodies of Catholic Irishmen killed by the British
Army; the crosses and priests in cassocks going to cemetery
at burial time; the old women in black, clutching rosaries,
weeping over the wooden boxes; the bitter faces of the
bereted men who marched in silence at their side. Nobody
paid any attention to the Cardinal's plea for moderation.
His being there, his simple presence, in all the old splendor
of an ancient liturgy, his crozier and mitre, his blessing
--this made him one of them, a Provisional IRA, and made
his blessing, a benediction to their guns. *What* he said
belonged to old-fashioned politics. His saying *anything at
all* before those coffins annealed his Church, despite its
politicians in the Vatican, to the men and women who
go down nightly into the streets to do battle.

The English past began five hundred years ago in Ireland.
That past in Ireland is present. The hated Protestant
hegemony in the North is symbolized by Catholics in terms
of "civil rights" and other conundrums, but the real issue
is simply *their* presence against *ours*, a foreign tribe in our
land, living off our lands robbed from us centuries ago. The
forty marshalls in green (color TV was needed to appreciate
this) who led the protest demonstrations after Black Sunday
did not say anything. They wore the green. They symbolized Ireland, free and Catholic.

10 War: Antiquity as Novelty

And the Ulstermen? "No Popery here." The Men of Orange,
one million hardy Protestants of Scotch-Irish descent whose
ancestors were invited by Cromwell to take those rich lands
in the north. They did well by them. Their politicians saw
to it that these lands could not be sold back to Catholics.
Identifying themselves fiercely with England, today they are
a figure without a ground. England has denied the Empire,
but the Empire lives on in Ulster, an embarrassing anachronism
to London.

101

The telepolitical show is totally tribal.

Every Ulsterman is enrolled in a lodge and when they march
on the Anniversary of the Battle of the Boyne, King James
loses again and King William and the Protestant cause
triumphs today and forever. Their banners and their
uniforms, their bands and their music, their throwing of
pennies over Fallchurch to the despised Catholics as the
parade sweeps by, flashes a conviction that Protestant
Ireland will endure, "the fairest gem in the crown of
the Queen." Even if England comes to terms with the
Irish Republic, the tragedy will not be settled. Protestant
Ireland will fight until killed and buried in the cemetery
of history. The evidence is in. Each man is right. Each
man is sure who he is and what he stands for.

The Irish Republican Army is vaguely Marxist. But Marxism
is an idea. It has nothing to do with Irish history, with
blood and life. The Catholic leaders disguise the conflict
under abstract slogans about "civil rights." But when the
Provisionals go out to die, they know it is a war of "religion"
--one tribe against another, "the hell with King Billy and God
Bless the Pope."   The battle in Ireland, truly a tragedy,
extends itself to an entire world tribalized electronically.

The Irish case, as illustrative of the telepolitical image, is
an instance of the return of the symbol and the death of
democratic debate. Everyone knows that tens of thousands
of Catholics, Irish and otherwise, drink tea; everyone
knows that tens of thousands of Protestants, Irish and
otherwise, drink beer. But beer as symbol of the Catholic
Thing is becoming a telepolitical reality that neither
Chesterton nor Belloc in all their contrived Catholic
booziness could make it in terms of their own literate
culture of the early century. The "wearing of the colors"
--a figure in Irish America thirty years ago, when little
Catholic girls were punished in parochial school if they
wore anything orange on St. Patrick's Day -- now mixes

itself through the media where Ireland has ceased to mean charming and harmless pixies but armed Catholic Provisionals and regrouping Protestant para-military units.

When men live mythically, all the evidence is *already* "in," collected. An image world stirs the most profound depths of the human spirit. While not necessarily contradicting reason, an image world sweeps reason into its own defence. It makes the content of debate and dialogue a mere instrument of existence. An image world, once the province of every tribe and clan, even of every family, is now the very substance of telepolitical reality.

The cautious and old-fashioned standards of most television executives as well as the literary education and objectivity --or, at least, sincere *pretension* to objectivity-- of most renowned television broadcasters have muted the power of television to work its magic upon the body politic. Sweet reasonableness reigns during the evening news when the masters introduce us to Belfast in flames. But what remains in the memory is Belfast in flames. The American television audience takes very well the tempered advice of Messrs. Smith and Sevareid, and Reasoner, and looks forward to hearing tomorrow at the same time their reasonable voices and seeing their reasonable faces.

But the same American television audience *does* remember Belfast in flames, the coffins, the crosses, the Green and the Orange. A million or more can die in Bangladesh and we pay little attention. But a dozen dead in Ireland brings back half-forgotten songs from an almost rejected youth. An interesting book might well be named "Television as an Instrument of Reaction." It would have all the charm and ambiguity latent in the difference between a book called "History as Television" and another called "Television as History."

Celtic tribalism,manifesting an astonishing staying power against the centralizing effects of mechanization, was nonetheless almost killed by the written word. Ireland's inability to make written Gaelic compete with written English, within the structure of a world in which the language spoken in the kitchen always gave way to the official language learned from books in the school, attests to the failure of smaller cultures to stand up to larger cultures in an age in which preponderance of hardware was equivalent to preponderance of power. That day is passing away but it passes with blood in its wake. The war in Ulster is not a civil war between a minority seeking political power over a majority within the structure of a national state. It is a war between two bitterly opposed tribes that are on stage before the whole world that identifies with one or the other tribe in the name of religion, or dissociates itself from both on the same basis.

The weakening of national unity everywhere in our time attests to the inward drive, the dispersing power, of the new media. Implosion produces discontinuity as an effect of simultaneity. The Catholic and Protestant American, disturbed by an Ulster that resurrects old bitterness and profound alienation, is forced to identify with one or the other tribe-- even if he does so uneasily and guiltily within this age of ecumenism. His uneasy identification has nothing to do with geography. The current discontinuity in life styles, in allegiances, transcends older commitments even as it fashions and images into existence knots of men and women who sharpen knives for a long night of apocalypse.

Both nationalism and internationalism are victims of the new technology. Electronics does to war what it does to politics-at-large. Electronics renders older categories obsolete even as it brings back ancient forms of political life in radically new structures.

Is Ireland what awaits us all?

104

Section II
Telepolitics

Part I
The War between Communication Systems

1 The Selling of the Pentagon: A Test Case

Barron's National Business and Financial Weekly, on March 29 1971, published a remarkable staff-written essay entitled "Broadcast License." The sub-title summed up *Barron's* thesis: "CBS has forfeited access to the nation's airways."

Barron's commented with tongue in cheek on Mr. Richard Salant's refusal to bend to the wave of criticism which engulfed CBS where he was president of the News Division. Salant stuck to his guns in defending the documentary "The Selling of the Pentagon." Neither the objections of the Vice President of the United States, the senior editor of *Air Force* magazine and the non-partisan citizens organization called Accuracy in Media could dent the moral self-righteousness of Mr. Salant. The intervention of the Vice President was simply a final blow done the freedom of the press by an administration which has scarcely veiled its hostility to the national news media.

"The Selling of the Pentagon" is a remarkable television production. It depicts a military industrial complex that glories in flexing the muscles of its own power. No one can doubt that the sheer poetry of power is sung eloquently in "The Selling of the Pentagon": the eerie blast of jet engines; the slick and trained violence of Green Berets in

hand-to-hand karate drill; the spit and polish of enlisted
seamen standing to attention as their gold-braided masters
salute smartly and welcome aboard typical civilian representatives of the American industry that made it all possible;
kids playing soldier at midwestern fairs, frolicking around
anti-aircraft hardware; the impressive figures running into
incredible billions spent on national defense; the lectures
on the Communist menace given by uniformed colonels
before grim and respectful citizens from mid-America; the
whole, bound together by Old Glory and the Star-Spangled
Banner --all of this, worked into a superb artistic catalyst,
gave the picture of a nation within a nation, of a mentality
frozen in the ideology of the cold war of the fifties, selling
itself to the America of the seventies.

In *Barron's* own account: "Here is CBS News' own dis-
passionate Roger Mudd: 'On this broadcast we have seen
violence made glamorous, expensive weapons advertised as
if they were automobiles, biased opinions presented as
straight facts. Defending the country not just with arms
but also with ideology, Pentagon propaganda insists on
America's role as the cop on every beat in the world.' "

Mudd made his most telling point when he made the Pentagon official he was interviewing admit that the scene depict-
ing American soldiers clearing a rice paddy of Viet Cong was
staged by the Pentagon. This is easily accomplished through
video editing and is in fact a process that is part and parcel
of the compressed daily news reporting of the major networks. The official's insistence that the staged skirmish was
typical of hundreds raised an epistemological issue which
the film ducked in its insistence that this lie was typical of
the PR tactics used by the Pentagon to sell itself to the
United States, and to ensure that Congress vote the proper
appropriations year after year.

It was revealed in the subsequent controversy that whirled
around "The Selling of the Pentagon" that some of the
answers given to Roger Mudd were actually answers to other

108

questions. At least one colonel sent by the Pentagon to lecture to civilian groups and one civilian who had been invited by the Pentagon to attend Army maneuvers were made to say things in answer to questions to which they had answered other things. The suspicion arose that CBS was as guilty of scissors, cut and paste politics as was the Pentagon itself.

The issues have been clouded because both sides of the controversy have insisted on arguing about issues. CBS accused the Pentagon of lying about a rice paddy raid. The Pentagon and its defenders have accused CBS of lying about the number of billions of dollars it spends and about the way in which CBS put together its supposed documentary. Both sides of the controversy have been caught with their pants down, although every second look at the issue indicates that the pants of CBS were caught much lower down on the legs of the body than were those of the Pentagon on its respective shanks.

Mr. Salant rejected the allegation that CBS had earlier been in the business of "financing a secret and illegal invasion of Haiti." According to the President of the News Division of the Columbia Broadcasting System, "We did not finance the planned invasion, we did nothing illegal, no significant amount of money ever inadvertently found its way to persons involved in the invasion plan. The Department of Justice found *no* unlawful activities on the part of CBS News --at one point the Treasury Department asked us *not* to withdraw from the project. But the short answer to the Vice President is that he is attacking a journalistic investigation that never became a broadcast about an invasion that never took place."

But "Project Nassau," CBS's name for the caper, *was* financed by CBS, according to the special subcommittee on investigation of the House Committee on Interstate and Foreign Commerce. CBS --the issue is detailed in the *Barron's* report-- provided the funds "for the leasing of

109

a 67-foot schooner which was to be utilized by the invasion force." CBS reimbursed the counter-revolutionaries for expenses incurred in the transportation of weapons to be used by them. During the preparation of the news documentary on Project Nassau, "CBS employees and consultants, intermingled and interacted with persons actively engaged in breaking the law." Large sums of money were made available to those individuals with no safeguards as to the manner in which these funds would be put to use. Events were set up and staged solely for the purpose of being filmed by the CBS camera.   The House Subcommittee found in CBS News "a shocking indifference to the real possibility that their organization and funds were being made use of to further illegal activities."

The morality of the issue could be argued on purely substantive grounds; e.g., (I) CBS thought an invasion of Haiti was a *good* idea and saw no reason why it should not forward this idea by financing men willing to put their lives on the line and furthering their cause by publicizing it; (2) CBS thought that the invasion was a *bad* idea because CBS disapproves of mercenary adventurers meddling in international politics and CBS decided to egg these men on with money in order to make them look irresponsible before the nation, all of this --of course-- under the cloak of reporting that which is; (3) CBS wanted to stage a good show.

Numbers 1 and 2 belong to the order of morality. One can confess transgressions against morality. Number 3 belongs to the order of art --or theater; good or bad art cannot be confessed. Art is not morality. But art can create its own morality by fashioning a new order of existence which would, thereby, necessitate the elucidation of its own morality.

Conversations about the ethics of the new media are extraordinarily premature because they are usually carried on by men who treat the new media as though they were extensions or developments of the old media.

The published document by the Synod of Catholic Bishops, Rome, 1971 on "Justice in the World" demanded that men be free from manipulation by media. This naive exhortation fails to take into account that media --all media-- are manipulatory in and of themselves. This includes the most basic of media seen as extensions of man: i.e., clothing, housing, transportation, tools, --in short, any technology. It all began with the caveman's axe. The farmer is servo-mechanism of his tools; the housewife is servo-mechanism of her vacuum cleaner; the soldier serves his rifle; mechanical man is the consequence of the image of the electronic world. Man creates his technologies and his technologies reciprocally form his environment. Causes mutually cause one another, according to Aristotle.

Telepolitics is a new order of being which is too young and too unsophisticated to have elaborated its own ethical code. Ethics always is the fruit of a long meditation on man's experience within some order of being. Telepolitics catapults him into a new order of reality within which he has not had enough time to think through whatever ethics might be implicit therein.

2 The Wrong Controversy about the Right Issue

CBS is innocent of these distinctions, because CBS, NBC, and ABC as well, have not thought through the principles of their own medium. Mr. Agnew insists on a kind of objectivity in the news media that is impossible. Agnew's partisanless morality suggests that he understands media as though they were glasses for limited vision. Granting that eyeglasses truly are a medium through which a man improves his eyesight, the Vice President and CBS have in common the naive assumption that the essence of television consists in simply reporting that which exists.

111

We have argued throughout this study that reporting is only a subsidiary function of television. Nonetheless, objectivity in reporting was presented in "The Selling of the Pentagon" controversy as the essence of the issue. It is by no means uninteresting that this moralism was advanced by CBS. This is the same CBS that butchered Mr. Henkin's statement about the duty of the Defense Department to inform the public concerning any possible increase in the Soviet threat to the United States. This is the same CBS accused by Accuracy in Media of having scissored and pasted Colonel MacNeil's speech into unrecognition.

Does not CBS understand that the genius of its own medium consists in bewitching into being *its own* order of existence, *its own* confrontation with truth? CBS did this in its criticism of the Pentagon. The Pentagon did this and continues so to do in *its* projection of *its own* image of itself.

Both CBS and the Pentagon are in the same business.

We all know that the makers of cheese or cars, or any consumer product, are severe competitors. CBS resents the Pentagon for being what CBS is: a communication system. The Pentagon is just as sophisticated in its pitch for what it believes as is CBS in its pitch for whatever it might believe. The question germaine to our study has nothing to do with adjudicating the substantive issues between the colossi of CBS vs. Pentagon.

What is important to an understanding of the new electronic world is the truth that two vast systems of communication have found themselves at war --one with the other.

Communications wars are nothing new. The whole history of propaganda attests to an attempt to let software do the work of hardware: i.e., get your enemy to surrender without firing a shot.

112

These wars were heated up with the invention of print. Leaflets, broadsides, rumormongering have been pressed into the service of politics, most especially the politics of war, since the early sixteenth century. "Tokyo Rose," "Lord Haw Haw," and Ezra Pound were World War II's most prominent exponents of communications war by radio. The fact that they were on the losing side might point towards a superior effectiveness and anonymity in these wars. The less you know that you are being bewitched by an "enemy," the more effective the spell.

These primitive wars between communication systems were organized and carried out against a recognizable and identifiable enemy "out there." The new electronic order has produced wars between communication systems whose effects blossom as would an atomic bomb *within* the psyche.

Advertising pioneered the way. The early buying and selling of newspaper space, which in turn bought and sold the eyes of subscribers, created and simultaneously occupied an inner space within the imagination of the reader. Advertising thus created disequilibrium, a tension that could only be resolved by buying the product. As Oscar Wilde put it, "the only way to get rid of a temptation is to yield to it." The competition between advertising wanting to occupy this internal space with its own prefabricated temptation was a war between communication systems.

The techniques of advertising formed the substance of the cold war of the fifties. McCarthyism and anti-McCarthyism, and even anti-anti-McCarthyism were image wars, each side using copious information to fashion a devil on all sides.

As Professor John Lukacs has pointed out, the McCarthyism of the fifties produced an internal panic about Communists in high and low places within the government which effectively hypnotized the nation. The misplaced enemy from within --there never was a ghost of a chance that Communism could take over the United States at that time-- ironically prevented the anti-Communist cause from squarely facing the Communist enemy from without, the growing military power of the Soviet Union and of China.

A peculiar irony of the internal nature of this era was the televizing of the Army-McCarthy hearings. The nation was divided between McCarthy and the Army. The implosive nature of television could not be more dramatically revealed. Russia was forgotten.

A striking parallel exists between the Pentagon-CBS communications war. Vietnam was lost in the shuffle.

CBS and its defenders, excepting the very far Left and the Communists, do not object to the Pentagon for being a military entity; they object to this military entity's having converted itself into a vast communication system.

The assumptive myth here is obvious: only non-political systems have a right to the airways. These non-political systems report what goes on "outside the airways." But it is a sin for this defense system to report about itself. The moral presuppositions are so patently evident that no one sees them. The Pentagon must not develop its own system of communication because soldiers are supposed to shoot people, not photograph the shooting. This is to forget that war today *is* a nexus of communication systems, of computerized technologies.

In Africa, when the "outs" want to take over a republic from the "ins," they seize the radio station. In a nation such as the U.S.A. with competing communication systems, power ultimately will fall to that communication system which can flash its message without interruption to the nation for a period of hours.

No system --CBS, Pentagon, or any other-- wants someone else's station on its screen. No power system can brook the intervention of any other power system.

114

Every communication system is political in that it alters man's relationship with man. Half in jest it has been suggested that NBC, ABC and CBS have replaced the Republican and Democratic parties. The jest has become reality when we are aware that the Pentagon has become a fourth member of the triumvirate --and in terms of raw power, the Pentagon can exist independently.

In the past communications software was sharply distinct from the hardware of weaponry. But the essence of the electronic revolution is the moving of information. This is most evident in computerized technology. Electronic hardware is essentially communicative. This means that hardware is not only at the service of software but that electronic hardware cannot function independently of a communication system which is built into its very structure. Moon landings directed from Houston are a striking instance of this principle. Therefore, the possession of an electronic communication system in and of itself is a potential weapon of war.

3 The New Kind of War

As stations proliferate into the tens of thousands in the declining years of the century, the monopoly on communication feared by the George Orwells in our midst who are haunted by visions of totalitarian control will be rendered a total impossibility. Communication wars between conflicting tribes who bid for the eyes and ears of the world will simply accentuate the decentralization already launched by the electronic revolution.

We predict that *nobody can win* this war in the post-modern world. The sheer weight of numbers of stations in competition will produce a kind of electronic stalemate as tribesmen tune off the foreign and hostile, jam hostile systems, and cradle themselves in their one electronic cosmion of meaning, in their own neuronic space.

The masters of the media will then cease attempting to "report" what goes on "outside the media" because counterattack will consist in being beamed-on by the enemy's own system. A vantage point from which old-fashioned "objectivity" could be achieved will have been virtually destroyed. Everybody will be under somebody else's electronic glare.

4 Revolutions: Left and Right

The Left gets better coverage on television than does the Right.

The New Left loathes old-fashioned liberalism but its political imagery has largely been inherited from our liberal past. A rhetorical facade links old and New Left and thus tends to mask the profound chasm separating the goals of both. Given that the media are largely in the hands of men who profess a vague liberal persuasion of an old-fashioned variety, the media tend to welcome the New Left because it is thought, or it was thought until very recently, that only differences in methods separated conventional liberalism from the new revolution of the Left.

This rhetorical anchor with the past is not available to traditionalist and other rightist political groups. They complain that revolutionary counterparts are made participants in the televised world whereas they are simply ignored or black-balled. In part this situation is rendered ambiguous by the vague sympathies marking the self-confessed friends of tradition. Why invite a man to your table when he considers the fare to be poison, when he believes that electronic technology is part of a plot to destroy nature and dehumanize man?

But Luddite sympathies, as we have argued, are equally prevalent in the New Left whose revolution today threatens to be splintered into agrarian communes fleeing the complexity of modern life.

116

A more sensible if commonplace explanation for the expulsion of the Right from the media is liberalism's ancient prejudice against *any* voice from right of center.

Possibly the swarm of rightist groups in the United States that lie in wait for their day --or God's judgment-- ought to count their blessings. *They* have not been emasculated as have the leftist heroes of the last decade.

Almost anybody over forty reading these lines will be astonished to know that the Reverend Gerald L.K. Smith, prominent in the thirties as the ally of Father Charles Coughlin against Roosevelt, is still going strong in his own corner of underground politics. His Easter pageant in Arkansas, centered around the statue of "the Christ of the Ozarks," continues to bring out the faithful. Millions upon millions do not know him. But he continues to be known and loved by tens of thousands who have remained faithful to him through four decades.

In contrast, the ten-minute shot on any leading national television show gives instant fame and just as instant boredom and obscurity. Any inveterate watcher of the *Today* show, America's morning symbolist, audio-visual collage, is familiar with the "ten-minute celebrity syndrome." We have become a nation of ten-minute celebrities --with high priests and priestesses of the media presiding over the liturgical rites.

During the 1968 Republican Convention in Miami, autograph hunters swarmed over a national TV newscaster as he walked side by side with the venerable Senator Everett Dirksen, a veteran of many years of senatorial service. The Senator was ignored. Walter Cronkite, Eric Sevareid, David Brinkley, Harry Reasoner, Barbara Walters, Dick Cavett, Johnny Carson are the new high priests of the liturgical rites of TV media. They dispense their media "states of grace" to the faithful whom they choose to interview, and their *ite missa est,* that's how it was, day, year, fade out.

5 Media Rejection by the Left

Rejection of the electronic media by the New Left and the Right is both visceral and intellectual: visceral in the Right and intellectual in the Left.

The voice of disgust against behaviorism in the political science community has been raised in recent years by professors identified explicitly or sympathetically with the New Left. Herbert Marcuse rejects Machiavelli's reduction of political science to pure power. Marcuse wants a modified Marxist and Freudian science capable of yielding power in the service of a new civilization built on the pleasure principle. Marcuse believes that technology represses man in his search for fulfillment. Technology enslaves.

As a Marxist, Marcuse attempts to disguise his romantic attachment to the quasi-Jacobite Captain Ludd, but his conviction reflects an increasing Manichaean rejection of television, the computer, and other proliferations of electronic technics. The logical conclusion to Marcuse's own insistence on pleasure is a defense of the new electronic biology that lulls men within its bosom even as it stimulates older erotic reality. The aged apostle of eroticism is altogether too much of a puritan, thanks to his Marxism, to tinker with such possibilities.

Marcuse is an implicit Aristotelian in that he always talks about science and technology in terms of politics. He will not be complimented if we say that he is implicitly Christian for so doing. Both the classical and Christian traditions insisted that technology ought to be controlled and bent to ethical considerations. Science, hence, had no autonomous right to develop independently of political goals. This theory, more sinned against historically than followed in practice, is hand-tailored for the Luddite rage of the New Left. But the New Left, despite Marcuse, has cut itself away from the very philosophical instruments it needs in order to articulate rationally its own rage. Today that rage is dissipating itself in mock burials of automobiles and internal combustion engines, in hatred against a world which is too slick,impersonal and mechanized.

A more sophisticated penetration of the history and ontology of technology would teach the New Left that the electronic revolution, like all revolutions, revolts against *something*; in this case against the older mechanical technology. Whereas the older technical order divided the universe into univocal instances which fall under a common model, permitting predictable results in the future, new technology tends by an inner dynamic to obliterate the future and to replace it by an abolition of both space and time as we have hitherto known them.

The older mechanical order was oriented toward work to be done. The newer technics find its center in the moving of information; the amazing "work results" produced by electronics are largely by-products of the capacity of the electronic to move information. Lunar "Eagle" landed on the moon thanks to information passed from the computer in "Columbia" to that in "Eagle" and from the information passed by the computer in "Eagle" to astronauts who read and interpreted. Without laboring the point, conquest of the moon indicates that the New Leftist blanket rejection of technology is largely a glance backward into the past.

6 Media Rejection by the Right

The more significant rejection of the new order is that of the far Right. We need think only of Governor George Wallace's phalanx in the election of 1968. Representing the older America of farms and small towns in rustic and homely virtue, the Wallace movement found its center in the older securities cherished by WASP America. It encountered, with both delight and surprise, northern allies, often Catholic

119

(Polish, Italian and Czech), in blue collar neighborhoods threatened by the dangerous nearness of the black man and menaced from within by pistoled violence stalking streets in the night. Wallace gained legitimacy through links with a quasi-mythological past filled by Southern plantations, lovely ladies, courteous gentlemen, and agrarian romanticism. His movement found all its power and encountered all its weaknesses in having blossomed almost totally without any appeal to the new world of mass communications dominated as suggested, by an Establishment foreign both to the ideals and the phobias proper to the American Party. As indicated, Mr. Wallace asked precisely those questions which are foreign to the rigid totalitarianism practiced by the masters of media.

By this we do not mean that George Wallace did not show up well on television. He performed superbly on *Meet the Press.* However, he performed as an effective, even cocky, fighter confronting enemies, not as a man who felt at home in the presence of Mr. Spivak and company. Wallace invaded foreign territory. The mass media remained foreign territory for the Wallace campaign to the very end of that campaign.

The older America compounded of ancestral pieties and latter-day fears used media with reluctance and was repaid for its integrity by a sound media thrashing in the final days of the campaign: "A vote for George Wallace is a vote thrown away." The very slogan turned one of four potential Wallace voters either away from the polls or into marking their ballots for Establishment candidates, Nixon and Humphrey.

But George Wallace had fingered the same national pulse of fear that throbbed through Mr. Nixon's campaign. The nation was running scared. Wallace was not able to parlay this into the fifteen million votes his most ardent followers predicted for him. He had bad media advice by men who hated the media anyway.

Richard Nixon learned his lesson from the narrow defeat he suffered at the hands of John Kennedy and could turn defeat into the narrow victory he won over Hubert Humphrey.

George Wallace also learned his lesson and learned it very well indeed. By early spring of 1972, Wallace was running fast in the primaries. He came from behind his desk with relaxed facial muscles. He was seen surrounded by relatives and children, romping and playing in those symbolic gestures whose appeal is their very commonality.

Wallace was not forced to change his political creed. He merely dimmed it slightly and thus permitted everyone to flash the fury or irritation of his own frustrations upon the Wallace image. In so doing, Wallace astounded the commentators and experts who had predicted that he would never cut deeply into the primaries north of the Mason-Dixon Line. George Wallace positively enjoyed being the gadfly of American politics. *They* are now sounding like George Wallace! Busing, high taxes, a groundswell of populist emotion by hard-hats, bluecollar workers, small businessmen, farmers, and even some Blacks who had been "messaged" to death, all formed a new wave which carried Wallace into Michigan and Maryland.

Uncle George has become the Archie Bunker of politics: let's tell it as it is. And Archie Bunker is the most popular character on TV today. Everybody has an uncle somewhere who sounds like Archie Bunker, although nobody wants to admit that the uncle is part of his own psyche. A WASP, Archie Bunker often sounds more like a northern Catholic ethnic. His appeal is universal. *I* would not talk that way out loud, but thank God that Archie does it! Thank God that Uncle George does it!

And then Arthur Bremer.

121

We do not know the fate, physical or political, of the wounded Governor of Alabama. But we do know enough about Arthur Bremer to at least limn his profile.

Spotted in Ottawa when Nixon met Trudeau, in Kalamazoo at a Wallace rally, living out of an automobile as he stalked his prey, Bremer was a loner who had vegetated in rooming houses and who was a mystery to those who knew him. A twenty-one-year-old child of the television generation, Bremer cut his long hair at the beginning of the year and assumed the role of a square. He was not known for entertaining strong political convictions. His apartment was littered with contradictory political symbols: George McGovern campaign literature and a Confederate flag.

Bremer gained instant fame with his gun. He was televised.

The wounded Wallace, hero of the new populist Right, is a living demonstration that the Right was viscerally correct in suspecting the new media. Without the new media its own hero would not have been gunned down in open daylight by a man who did not seek the shelter of a distant window with a high-powered rifle, but kleig lights, the close-in revolver, and immediate capture --all televised.

Television has created the lonely killer. (We do not rule out the possibility of a plot but the plot could only be executed by the loner who sought not safety and money but electronic fame.) If you cannot make it to the screen on your own, you can always do so with a gun. Possibly all campaigns in the future will be fought out within the electronic theater, far from the violence of the streets. Possibly the only answer to televised violence is to get both the candidates and the camera off the streets. This would make for a very "cool" political life indeed. It would also be another nail driven into the coffin of American politics as we have known it in the past.

7 The New Praetorians

The far Right, like the far Left, has been quite logical, although suicidal, in rejecting Telepolitics or in using Telepolitics only with great reluctance. Rightist politics conjures up a world reminiscent of the older agrarian America marked by thrift, hard work, Fourth of July parades, and visualized superbly in Grant Wood's painting, *American Gothic.*

Let us be careful that we understand the sundering issues involved here. If the good life is simply America of the past, then the new media, given their enormous power to transform the social fabric, must appear as diabolic. The reactionary position, as defined, will traffic with electronic media in an attitude reminiscent of Pope Pius XI's quip about bargaining with the devil for the salvation of one soul.

Let us not misunderstand the issue: the radicals and reactionaries in our midst are committed to a way of life which has *no place* for and in television.

Radicals and reactionaries could possibly accomodate the new media to their cherished ways of life. But they have shown little patience in attempting to understand the philosophical nature of the electronic revolution.

It is significiant that Marshall McLuhan is damned by the Left as being a covert traditionalist hankering after the twelfth century and by the Right as being the apostle of barbarism. If supposedly sophisticated critics of the media cannot get their categories straight when they attempt to evaluate this illustrious Canadian literary critic who has bent his energy and talent to understanding the age electronic, we cannot expect insight of men who still think in terms of the nineteenth century.

The attitude of media rejection was adumbrated in a vague and amorphous fashion in the fifties by those many Americans who refused to buy television sets. They were convinced that the invasion of the idiot box would destroy family unity or debase the national taste. These were the fifties, age of the famous silent generation: "elitist groups" baked salvation in brown bread out of the house oven, gloried in the absence of antennas over their rooftops, made a mystique out of large families and deified the intimacy of family and the kingship of the child. Most of these groups, initially traditionalist if not reactionary, have either disappeared or, through the curious alchemy of history, have converted themselves into one form or another of religious establishmentarianism. They helped prepare, however, the advent of the Praetorian guard of Mr. Wallace.

To the degree to which media can get this older America over this moment of crisis, media will be used by the Praetorians. Although they look forward to the day when this will no longer be necessary, it is doubtful that any Praetorian guard can govern today without making itself master of the electronic media.

Part II
Telepolitics as Theater

1 The Nature of Telepolitical Theater

If theater is an attempt to see life clearly and to see it whole;
if theater is the holding of a mirror up to nature; if theater
is ideas in conflict so that men may gain a heightened awareness of the problems of their time and possible solutions;
if theater is the suspension of judgment primed by a will
that consciously pretends that what is not real is real,
then television is *not* theater.

But if theater is a parade, a pageant, a circus, a show, a
diversion to make men forget the unpleasant realities of
everyday existence; and if theater is a ritualized and controlled
act which sweeps an audience into the vortex of total
participation, as did the Roman circus, then television *is*
indeed theater.

Theater as willed pretense is in glittering opposition to the
messiness of existence, an effort to find --or create-- some
order in all that chaos. But theater as arena simply sweeps
away the unsatisfying discontinuity of reality in order to
stylize life and thus blur, even obliterate, the difference
between seeming and being.

The ancient image of the arena comes fully into its own
today.

125

2 Telepolitical Man: The Kennedy Style

The Kennedy style of the famous thousand days possessed a glitter that enchanted the world --and covered up a stunning failure, according to older values.

John Kennedy failed to achieve his own domestic program. The war against poverty was deferred to the Great Society of L.B.J. Kennedy bungled badly on the international stage: the tragedy of the Bay of Pigs; the progressively deteriorating situation in Vietnam; the solid Soviet success before the Berlin Wall; the impossible flirtation with revolutionary movements in South America and opposition groups in Portugal and Spain --all of these suggested a political eclecticism whose diverse elements were never forged into unity.

Nonetheless, President Kennedy was a superb success by the standards of the newer Telepolitics. He gained the hearts of West Berliners by identifying with them in his famous "Ich bin ein Berliner" speech. He gripped the imagination of South America by simply proclaiming the Alliance for Progress, which in practice has been a notorious failure. Touch football, fifty-mile walks, a new mysticism of youth in the White House and an America that must "get moving" again, took the place of legislative successes. The world was entertained and edified by vicarious participation in the thrilling "inner" life of the entire Kennedy clan. There never had been a more dramatic American success story.

The easy, cool mastery of TV by Mr. Kennedy never shone more luminously than it did in that first televised debate with Richard Nixon. These debates have been dissected by a sufficient number of surgical masters of media. One man came through and the other man did not. There is little doubt that this very act of coming through on TV gained the election for John Kennedy. That he died as publicly as he lived was both symbolic and symptomatic of the new order.

From silk-hatted youthful exuberance over television on Inauguration Day to blood-spattered death on Zapruder's film, President Kennedy spawned a style the success of which reached beyond his own death to catapult into tragedy his brothers Robert and Ted.

3 Telepolitical Funerals

Funerals have come back into fashion in the age of Telepolitics. This significance is generally lost because the melioristic ideology inherited from earlier decades of the century suppressed the awesome and overbearingly personal character of death.

A man's total biography is closed with his death. Funerals are a dirge to ultimate tragedy, to personality frustrated in ripeness. The Age of the Child played down the old; even today it is a crime for a grandmother to look like one. Outside media, kiddie orientation still holds the day. *Inside* politicized media kiddies cannot compete with death.

The politics of death is part of a new order of existence. The political funeral is a symbol for every home in the industrialized world.

Chancellor Konrad Adenauer's funeral was marked by a manly and martial air, muted, reflecting the chastened vigor of the new Germany.

The Montreal funeral of murdered Quebec labor minister Pierre Laporte, attended by Canada's Prime Minister Trudeau protected by armed soldiers on rooftops, gave dramatic emphasis to the War Measures Act proclaimed only a few days before, and to the P.M.'s promise that those who had "no mandate but terror" would not prevail.

For the second time in his political career, Trudeau's great personal courage was to come through on TV. Those watching his arrival for the funeral were reminded of the eve of his election when, in front of the reviewing stand at the St-Jean Baptiste parade, riots broke out, and --while all the other dignitaries scurried for cover--Trudeau flung off the bodyguard attempting to protect him and stood alone in the box. Now, attending the funeral of a man who, but by the grace of God, could have been him, he showed similar courage, and TV was again there to record it, following him as he alighted from his limousine and walked across crowded Place d'Armes to the church. After all, it was Trudeau whom the terrorists most hated, for it was he who most symbolized a united Canada.

In all Canadian history, there can be few more dramatic events than this funeral of Pierre Laporte. The suspense of watching for a movement in the crowd combined with the effort to understand the horror of the death of the man in the coffin inside. Why Laporte? Why had Laporte, a man of intelligence and goodwill who in many ways summed up the best of the new Quebec, been killed in the name of that new Quebec? And the nature of his murder? Strangled by the chain that held the religious medallion around his neck, as if part of some Satanic ritual calculated to flaunt the faith by which his people had lived for more than four hundred years. What did this portend for the future?

The funeral bells of Notre Dame Church that fall day tolled more than the death knell for a good man; they mourned the end of serenity in Canadian political life which had not been afflicted with an assassination in one hundred and two years.

Martin Luther King's funeral gestured the frustrations and bitterness of a race told to "dream a dream" by the man it buried. Among the hushed mourners surrounding the chiseled black beauty of King's widow, a blackness deepened by her widow's weeds, were all the leading

128

presidential aspirants of both Republican and Democratic parties. Telepolitics had made guilt public by its corporate liturgical expression in Dr. King's burial. All candidates for the office of President had to testify to their own guilt in the murder of Black America's leader. The issue has nothing to do with personal guilt, of course. The personal today is the *persona,* the mask probed by Jung, celebrated 3,000 years ago in the Greek theater.

Is Telepolitics changing our understanding of what it means to be a person?

Does total participation in the public rites of the forum make personhood an act of symbolic communion rather than a stance of solitary and individualistic incommunicability?

The nation sprang to attention when it heard muted drums, caissons and the slap of rifle wood and steel against hands and shoulders as uniformed men carried Eisenhower to a hero's Valhalla. The nation mourned publicly for four days in a fashion not found in death as encountered in a typical middle-class affluent American family in real life.

Robert Kennedy riding in death to lie next to his brother in Arlington; Eisenhower on the plains of Kansas; Martin Luther King reposing in the bosom of his people; America suffered and celebrated three public burials in one year. America suffered because it mourned and America celebrated because it mourned and America celebrated because its mourning was liturgical, a rite exercised, done. The national effect was cathartic.

Death, hidden away as an indecent and pornographic intrusion into "life," came back with a vengeance into the public forum, thanks to Telepolitics.

129

4 In the Creation of the Image

The ritual of death points to the new sense of *persona*
marking the statesman. Old-fashioned politics, unobfus-
cated by ideology, insisted that the job of the magistrate
was to govern. Political success was measured in terms
of the politician's ability to govern well. This task involved the fusion of a host of virtues and --possibly-- a
vice or two.

Participation in government, within the framework of
democratic dogma, was composed of the two dimensions:
the subordinate, be he ward heeler or cabinet member,
had to interpret the will of his superior but also had to
assume a limited authority and take responsibility for acts
falling within his own competence.

Today the first question asked of a potential candidate for
high office looks to his saleability, his image, his charismatic
character, his ability as an actor to project a cool image.
His capacity to govern is secondary. If he does not look
good, he will not be elected.

Leaders, therefore, are expected to see their chief role as
that of symbol maker and symbol manipulator. We need
only think of the grand style of Charles de Gaulle, the
exciting style of John Kennedy, the folksy style of
President Eisenhower, the patrician style of Pierre Trudeau,
the severe style of Francisco Franco, and the pragmatic
style of Richard Nixon, to realize that political success today
is one with successful theater. In part this accounts for the
otherwise inexplicable emergence into American political life
of professional actors. The distance we have come can be
measured in terms of the rise in the scale of value of the
actor from mountebank to seer.

Lyndon Johnson's decision not to run for re-election was
triggered by the famous "credibility gap." By every criterion

of older politics, L.B.J. was a howling success, but he failed to find a telepolitical image. In extra-electronic life men move from cajoling to persuading, from sweet reasonableness to ire. The attitudes are one with human relationships as we experience them outside media. But the electronic theater demands aesthetic consistency and Johnson could never find it. Telepolitics ruined him, not politics.

If the role of the leader has become that of symbol bearer, the democratic process itself has also been altered deeply. Participation involves interpretation of orders and the assumption of responsibility. These older political roles have not disappeared, but are being subordinated rapidly to participation in the charisma of the leader.

This has very little to do with ideology. We witness a revival of the old Roman institution of the *princeps,* a sweeping of political talent into the vortex of personal charisma, Sorensen and Schlesinger at the service of the clan.

Doctrinal convictions had nothing to do with the rallying of the faithful after Martha's Vineyard. Sorensen and McNamara helped with Senator Kennedy's television apologia not because they believed that the Senator was potentially a better governor than they were or a brighter idealogue, but because he was a dynastic symbol, the man who had "picked up the standard." We are witnessing the decay of the monarchical and the return of the dynastic principle to the political arena.

5 The Return of the Dynasts

In a classical sense of the term *monarchy*, one man governs. He may have received the diadem of power from a family but could equally have emerged from the anonymity of the masses. He might well be the darling of the Praetorian guard, or he might stand as gray eminence behind a weak throne. One man rule is monarchical and is not based necessarily on heredity. We need only think of Napoleon Bonaparte.

In a dynastic situation --we use the term in its strict political sense-- the man governing may govern well, poorly, or indifferently, but he always governs ultimately --thanks to the name he bears-- to his having come forth from a family, be that family royal or aristocratic.

Andrew Jackson broke the old Virginia dynasties in the United States. For better than two-thirds of a century since Jackson, few Americans occupying high office, and none occupying the Presidency, possessed the mantle of power because they had inherited it.

We speak of "inheritance" here not in the strictly legal sense attaching to the word in European kingdoms, but in the social and charismatic sense belonging to the mere possession of an illustrious name that marks all aristocratic republics. One governs, in such political orders, because "the standard" has been passed to him, because "the mantle" has devolved upon his shoulders. The older democratic road to the fullness of power symbolized by the White House, open for a century to any poor boy who could rally the people to his cause or who espoused theirs, has not been eliminated today but is rapidly being closed.

It is increasingly difficult for a nobody to capture the democratic masses. The new dynasts are the darlings of the plebians. The stylized political *persona* is not an individual any more than a Kennedy is an individual. This stylized persona must be married, must have children, a happy wife, and parents. Increasingly, he must have grandparents. He must be a paradigmatic person, Mask of the Race.

132

The Methodist church served by Senator McGovern's father in Avon, South Dakota, gone to seed, was refurbished by the Lions Club when it looked as though George McGovern might go somewhere in American politics. A future demands that a past be created or --at very least-- tidied up.

Telepolitics has brought back the family to the political forum. The paterfamilias was a political disadvantage in the immediate American past. He suggested a series of interests which were not totally identified with the commonweal. Most politicans, of course, enjoyed or suffered family life. This dimension, however, was draped from public scrutiny during the classical years of democratic liberalism. The invasion of political life by charismatic ideologies promising salvation on earth made the family a peripheral embarrassement to the *Parousia*. The family lives of Marx, Lenin, Trotsky, Stalin and Hitler were kept hidden from the elect. These men were simply the carriers of salvation.

Leaders of totalitarian movements, hiding their bourgeois domestic privacy, presented themselves publicly as lonely and ascetic saints, dedicated to a new gospel. (A wife cuts down the worship given the hero.)

The lonely hero is politically viable only within two social situations: he is the solitary repository of the salvation of the whole people with whom he has contracted exclusive nuptials; or he bears the solitary asceticism of a celibacy celebrated as a higher way of life by a society in which monogamous familial life is the norm. In the first instance, Fuehrer finds his Bride in the *Volk*. In the second instance, the statesman exemplifies an ideal of celibacy beyond the norm, Hitler and Salazar were "celibate" heroes, public sacrifices to their marriage with the people.

The television set squats in a house lived in by a family. The entire family watches the tube. Often watching television is the only time an entire family is gathered together in the same room. Beamed back upon this private family assemblage is the paradigmatic family of the new public figure. He is just like us --after all-- isn't he? The new plebians vicariously participate in a new patrician order. Mmes. Eisenhower, Kennedy, Johnson and Nixon everywhere dispense largesse and feminine bountifulness. Entire families swarm through media in the Inauguration Balls. Mr. Nixon does not swear in the members of his Cabinet. He swears in father, mother and children, even a cabinet minister's wife with a broken leg! This is an age of sexual permissiveness for the masses, but not for the masters.

Telepolitics moves us back into an order reminiscent of the classical aristocracy of the Roman Republic. Plebians are content with being brilliant and well-paid technicians or they marry the new patricians. Nixon marries Eisenhower and Percy marries Rockefeller. Stratification moves upwards. Social mobility retreats back into anonymity and atomic individuality, unbuttressed by familial ties. Blood, once again, takes precedence over brains, but blood --holding the power-- acts as a vortex into which the brains are swept. Political alliances are effected by contrived marriages. The ancient principle of dynastic politics, associated historically with the house of Hapsburg, now becomes a commonplace in a public order demanding that statesmen be paradigmatic men: of family with wife of equal substance, coming out of a recognizable past, moving towards a predictable future.

Telepolitics has murdered democratic individualism. The U.S.A. today lives dynastically and does so most powerfully in those very circles that preach the democratic myth.

The dynastic Senator Ted Kennedy is possibly best known in and out of Congress for his insistence upon equality under the law. Kennedy took to himself the older American democratic symbolism. He has not protested any contra-

134

diction between his public commitment to legal equality and the legal tenderness proffered him after Miss Kopechne's death because of his dynastic position. The issue has nothing to do with any supposed hypocrisy on the part of the Senator. The issue is one with the new symbolic, and therefore universal, role conferred upon all public figures within the new Telepolitics.

Plato insisted that the political order is man "writ large." Expressed in terms of depth psychology, Plato's insight means that there is an ambiguity in the human psyche which can never be resolved, a tension between individual personhood and citizenship. This very failure of resolution is a mainspring of the movement from solitary life to public participation in the rites of the forum. The image of the dynastic father must be sufficiently familiar to us all that we might identify with him.

The public man's family coincides with ours --so, too, his ideals and goals. We sense ourselves participants in his life and in the larger life of his idealized family. But the image must be sufficiently broad and all-encompassing that participation leaves intact a sense of psychological distance.

The leader is greater than we are. His family, while a complete family as is our own --or (and this is more effective) as we wish that our own family might be-- purifies the human situation and thus lifts us above the paltriness of our own present existence, filled --as it is-- with imperfections and failures.

The common expression, often heard of a politican, "he is just like the rest of us" both means what it says and means exactly the opposite: were he just like the rest of us, it would never occur to us to say so!

6 The Marriage of Media

The capacity to project both intimacy and distance is endemic to television as an electronic form.

We abstract here from the controversial insistence that we participate intensely in television because we "fill in" a blurred image on the screen. The medium itself operates within a host of other media and the total effect of television is conditioned by these environmental media. A televised football game seen in a bar is simply not the same environment as a televised political address seen in one's home. The intimacy which is one with television itself is buttressed enormously because the tube is located in our family room. Televised imagery prohibits the agonizing over problems and the nail chewing that lost Mr. Bush from Texas a seat in the United States Senate.

We do not wish agonizing in our family rooms, especially after a long day at shop or office. The politically-imaged figure must project into our lives as *then lived, at that moment,* one of relative personal relaxation mingled with impersonal, objective expectancy. During prime time the American family is most "familial," most united and that union is one of repose. The intimacy achieved must transcend even while it englobes us. It must wrap us into a legendary and mythological projection of what we want to be. In a nation still overwhelmingly dominated by the monogamous family, despite the heavy attacks launched against that institution today, mythological projection of the viewer structures itself into an idealized familial form at the *precise moment* --prime time: six to nine in the evening-- when the family comes closest to achieving the inner unity that its members long for in the depths of their otherwise alienated hearts.

The gnostic leader of the totalitarian thirties as well as the democratic leader of the American myth of the past hundred years, both burning with the charisma of salvation,

136

give way to the archetypal family which both stoops to conquer and lifts to exploit.

7 The Family and Politics

Curious shifts in the political wind, experienced by everybody but rarely articulated consciously, bear witness to the return of the dynastic principle in American public life. The dynastic has been able to creep back into politics because democratic mythology insists that the United States is an egalitarian republic in which each man, in the solitary loneliness of the election booth, votes his conscience according to a naked consideration of the abstract worth of the candidates. The myth operates as a smoke screen.

All private life, of course, is dynastic to some degree. The vast majority of men and women everywhere in the Western world spend the better part of their lives coming out of families, raising families, working for their children, marrying them, burying parents, and being buried by their own offspring.

Any objective observer of the political history of the past two hundred years must be astonished at the power of the Enlightenment and of the Revolution, of democracy, to abolish the family from political life and restrict the franchise to individuals. This split of familial life from political institutions, a novelty in the backdrop of the total two-thousand year sweep of Western Man's history, was a reaction against royal and dynastic government. The split also reflected the conviction that public and private life were two separable components in society.

Possibly England's retention of the monarchy as symbol, after all effective ground of power for that institution had been washed away through two and one-half centuries of parliamentary supremacy, was an implicit recognition

137

of the need to institutionalize the family and hence to render public the private dimension of life. This logical contradiction has been psychologically fruitful because the royal family in England is the one rallying focus of continuity in a society that has been profoundly altered since World War II. Second only to Scandinavia in its exultation of free sex, England has seen to it that its Royal Family has stood as a symbol of domestic fidelity. The seed plot of democratic socialism was England's Fabian movement. But, Great Britain supports a most non-democratic institution to the tune of hundreds of thousands of pounds a year.

Inchoately grasping the truth that monolithic industrial standardization demands a counterweight, England has cherished and maintained the ritual coronation of its sovereigns, so that this act is today the most majestic and colorful and magical political event in the Western world.

Even the crude and paleolithic television of 1953 could not hide --it rather accentuated-- the symbolic marriage of a shabby nation with its past splendor in the person and figure of the Queen.

The dynastic principle in England has a brilliant future provided that its carriers have the intelligence to wed it to telepolitical imagery. It has no future at all if it sinks into the plebian and democratic style adopted by the crowned heads of Scandinavia and Holland. What the masses want today is more pomp and circumstance and they want it personalized.

8 Mr. Humphrey: A Case in Point

The divorce between public and private life worked for generations. But let us now return to Mr. Humphrey who ran his campaign in 1968 on "the issues." As an old-fashioned politician hewn out of wood already aged in the days of Franklin Roosevelt, Humphrey hammered his convictions into every home in the nation. He breathed conviction and enthusiasm in every public address, televised or not.

But issues by themselves no longer win elections, not in the age of Telepolitics. Images win elections. And the primeval image, dragged back into a generation that thinks in terms of sexual liberty and the abolition of the family, has been the family, writ large.

Solitary liberty and sexual abandon are truly goals of millions today, but they cannot be projected electronically because they cannot be dreamed *corporately*. These ideals are divisive and non-participatory. A conscious liberation for a solitary individual demanding liberty is as incapable of electronic projection as is the successful projection of the individual politician arguing issues in the abstract. Individualism is as cerebral as is *Playboy*, as calculating as a computer.

When Mr. Humphrey, a very warm man, ran his campaign for the Presidency, he was not thinking of the new religion of individual expression which he probably does not understand and almost certainly rejects. He was thinking in terms of an older individualism --father of the youth rebellion today-- that insisted mythologically that every potential voter weigh the issues in his mind and cast his vote in terms of convictions achieved personally, hence within the untouchable prism of the democratic soul.

Solidarity was achieved by the free grouping of individuals into political parties, trade unions and churches. Democratic mythology historically had to compromise with the doctrine of party loyalty. Both point to the perennial tension between tribal identity and personal responsibility. The insistence upon party loyalty from the faithful, linked with the democratic myth that each man must weigh his vote in the light of conscience, constitutes what logicians call a contradiction. Nonetheless, this contradiction rendered

139

possible the very going-on of American life throughout one hundred and fifty years. There are very few indeed who here would prefer logic to history.

Bossism is party loyalty carried to its logical extreme. Bossism is the American equivalent to the Roman institution of the *princeps*, itself an unofficial institution as is its contemporary counterpart. Mr. Humphrey in the campaign of 1968 was consistent in his ambiguity, as has been the tradition he incarnated. Appealing to the loyalty of the democratic masses, he nonetheless insisted upon arguing contentiously to "the nation" in terms of "the issues." Party chieftain Humphrey sensed that personal loyalty and affection extended from standard bearer to party and not from candidate to nation. To the Democrats he pleaded loyalty; to the nation he pleaded reason. In so doing, Mr. Humphrey acted in the very best --and ambiguous-- traditions of American political life.

In late October, the Humphrey advertising men produced the movie, *The Mind Changer.* In the words of Joe McGinniss:*

"It was awful in many ways. It showed Hubert Humphrey and Edmund Muskie crawling down a bowling alley in their shirt sleeves. It showed Humphrey wearing a stupid fisherman's hat and getting his lines snarled on a lake near his home and it took shameless advantage of the fact that he has a mentally-retarded granddaughter. It was contrived and tasteless. But it was the most effective single piece of advertising of the campaign."

Humphrey almost won the election on the basis of this film; he emerged, finally, as a family man and a warm and good one at that. This familial image, truly iconic in its *universal projection of man,* writ large, appealed directly to the entire nation and not simply to the "party." It cut below reason; it hit the heart. Hubert Humphrey could

The Selling of the President (Pocket Books, N.Y., 1970) p. 141

140

truly use, and be believable, the royal "we." That he used
it too late is a lesson well digested by the magicians who
make candidates today in the United States of America.

9 The Royal "We"

"Where's Jackie?" someone in the crowd shouted.
*"Mrs. Kennedy is organizing herself," the President said. "It
takes longer, but of course she looks better than we do when
she does it." The crowd loved this, and roared its approval.*
Words of President John F. Kennedy quoted in *The Vantage
Point.* *

Now there is something extremely curious --as well as funny--
about the form of President Kennedy's language in referring
to his and his wife's appearance. "She looks better than *we*
do." Why the contrived "we" when there is no doubt that
he really means "I?" But did he, after all, *really* mean "I?"
There can be no question of Kennedy appealing to the majestic
impersonality of his office, symbolizing its union with all the
people through the ceremonial "we." Nor, in the context,
is there any question of Kennedy's sweeping his audience
into himself, investing it with a corporate personality. He
did not mean that Jackie looked better than all of them,
the crowd plus himself, taken together. Nonetheless, he used
the old royal "we" in a matter as personal and even idiosyn-
cratic as clothing.

Why the royal "we" in a nation that gloried in shaking itself
free of kings and potentates and of power based on the
simple charisma of blood? Why the "we" in a nation that
so suspected the familial and that so exalted the lonely and
individualistic "I" that its very constitution forbids acceptance
by public officials of a title of nobility?

The Vantage Point, Lyndon Baines Johnson (Holt, Rinehart and Winston,
New York, 1971) page 1

Nobody has commented to our knowledge, on how the royal "we" crept back into political parlance in our time. It began with John Kennedy who used it lavishly and who reverted to the older "I" only when he confronted the hostile Veterans of Foreign Wars. Today every candidate for office and every officeholder, down to that of dog-catcher, uses the papal and royal "we."

Initially the royal "we" pertained to dynastic monarchies. The king's use of "we" symbolized his conviction that he spoke not in his own name as an individual but in the name of the dynasty whose head he was, the dynasty which summed up the kingdom, the *regnum*.

The notion is older than Sir John Fortescue who first articulated it legally and philosophically in his panegyric of the laws of England. The king was the head of the political body. As used by popes the "we" meant "Peter and I," thus separating the holder of the Papacy from any individual-istic claims to personal charisma in what he said or did.

The royal "we" has been built into the very grammatical structure of a number of western languages as a mark of solemnity in him who speaks and as a sign of respect and even affection in him who responds. The entire history of this usage points to the deepest meanings of *legitimacy*. No man in political power was legitimate in and of himself; he inherited his legitimacy either through blood or, in ecclesiastical politics, through the apostolic succession.

The age of democratic individualism effectively did away with this royal "we" in secular politics. The liberal division of functions between the head of state and the head of government relegated to the former a shadow of the older legitimacy. We need only think of the English, Scandinavian, or Japanese "sovereigns." But the heads of government in these and other European and Asiatic nations speak in terms of the "I": premiers are responsible, not kings, for the political destinies of their countries.

Democratic insistence on the impersonality of institutions, on their theoretical openness to anyone within the democratic "nation," was summed up early in the game by Napoleon's statement that every French foot soldier carried a *maréchal*'s baton in his knapsack.

The collapse of democratic institutions in Europe after World War I did not restore the old royal "we." Mussolini, Hitler and Stalin governed as supreme egos. Adolf Hitler always used the first person singular when he really meant it. He used the plural only when he consciously articulated his mystic union with the entire German *Volk*. His usage was typical of his age, even of those nations that resisted the totalitarian dream.

Franklin Roosevelt --an aristocrat with a venerable family tradition-- rarely used the "we" when he enunciated policy. Today, however, as indicated, even candidates for the most petty offices use the "we."

Why did the age of democratic individualism permit great figures to emerge who spoke in their own name? Why did Fascist and Communist totalitarianisms do the same? Winston Churchill, an aristocrat from an illustrious family, never presumed to the "we;" this was reserved for the monarch. But there is not an American reader of these pages who cannot remember his local candidates for city hall, yesterday, under questioning by the media, who did not hesitate to speak of "our program for this playground" and "our thoughts on racial imbalance."

The questions posed, as well as the anomalies, suggest the following: the age of democratic individualism removed from aspirants for political life any formal legitimacy for the roles they played; they made it thanks to their own talents. With the collapse of democratic institutions earlier in the century and the rise of totalitarianism, the "leader" governed simply through personal and quasi-mystical charisma. Despite the vast differences between

143

democracy and totalitarianism, both share in common the conviction that politics is a public realm about which men, through the use of their individual reason, can discover "the truth."

But relativism has been a national religion in North America. When politicians speak their mind today they must do so in the name of something larger than their own personal capacity to understand and resolve the issues. The proposition must seem paradoxical: naked rationality is no longer the mark of reasonableness; the man "who knows all the answers" is considered irrational. The candidate cannot orate clothed in symbolism of the rationality of the Revolution of 1775. He cannot act as though he were a living middle term mediating a syllogism moving towards a supremely rational solution to a living problem. Nobody believes in these things anymore.

The return of the "we" in American politics indicates a convergence of two truths: (1) politicians, taken in the large, and by the handful, do not dare to advance what they believe *in the name simply of their own belief;* they must speak in the name of something larger than themselves; (2) this "larger dimension" can no longer be the abstractions of the older Revolution today hardened into a venerable conservatism; the typical political and social institutions of the nation are decaying and no longer command the assent of the community. The concrete symbolism that once surrounded the abstract principles of democratic republicanism has died except in the camp of the northern and mid-western Right where it still commands a visceral response.

The Lincoln Memorial in all the cold splendor of its abstract dedication to democratic equality is also totally concrete, bound up with the messiah who sent the troops marching to the sound of *The Battle Hymn of the Republic.* But that day is now past. The cold flame of equality can kindle a fire in nobody's heart. The nineteenth century is gone forever. The new order is totally "we" oriented.

The "we" was as foreign to the nineteenth century as it was to the abstract purity of the revolutionary fanaticism of Robespierre. Nor, to swing across the channel, does the "we" point to the politics of proscription of the great conservative, Edmund Burke. The United States today --torn to pieces by warring tribes and stalked by a profound doubt concerning the viability of its own inherited instit- utions-- is neither conservative eighteenth century England nor democratic eighteenth century France.

The royal "we" in our time adumbrates a legitimacy based neither on individualistic reason --rejected by the common relativism: "your opinion is as good as mine" --nor on the older sacrosanct character of republican institutions, today under attack everywhere within the spectrum of American society. "We" is a symbolic gesture. "We" speaks out of a passion for a communion in existence which antedates politics and which takes the pressure of personal responsibility off the backs of the individual politician who hungers for legitimacy.

The return of totally-involved kinship groups, pressured into existence by electronics, is bringing back a politics based on family and blood. This is most especially true of those politicians with neither blood nor family but expec- tations of both. The "we" --as they climb up the political ladder from obscurity-- is more frequently on their lips than on those of men already settled in life. The "we" of these solitary souls, pretending to a ghostly dynasty and legitimacy, is a cry that surges out of the depths of human nature, a nature demanding that men come from somewhere, go somewhere, be accompanied by someone, and represent more than the pale shadow of a handful of ideas as they pass through life. All institutions of the old political order collapse. The family as myth remains and grows. The family is finding a new moment of electronic glory.

145

The family, whose espoused defenders on the Christian
Right often hate television, has been brought back by
television. The reasons for this resurgence of dynastic
politics are formally one with television itself. The lonely
individual preaching "the Truth" is a "hot" gestalt. We need
only think of the Rev. Charles Coughlin, the "Radio Priest"
of the thirties, a voice speaking hope through a little box
to millions during the Great Depression. His personal talent
was welded to a "hot" medium capable of exploiting his
genius to the limit. (Fr. Coughlin was a political flop when
he took to the stump and faced live audiences campaigning
for Rep. William Lempke in 1936.)

The radio heats up tribal warfare in Africa. The radio
--heard by millions of Americans on their way to work
early in the morning-- tells The Truth crudely. Television
calms that truth down in the evening news. A man
surrounded by wife and children after a day's work will never
embrace any message promising salvation. Such a man,
seeking relaxation and entertainment even in his "serious"
television watching, is cool by his very situation. If he
wanted to heat himself up he would have left the house
and found the nearest tent revival. Familial communion and
participation, when domesticity runs smoothly, cool in
and of themselves. The politician from nowhere and out
of nobody with a message to sell cannot sell it over television
in the evening, not because people hate him but because
electronic media cannot project him without rendering
him grotesque and intolerably abrasive. Remember: it
is 6:00 to 9:00 in the evening. The cooling effect of the
electronic tube is buttressed by a score of familial media
that massage the viewer. Lonely individualism is not
welcomed at these moments of repose.

10 Double Political Standards

The political hot-gospeler of the older democratic tradition
is as obsolescent as the vendor of cure-all medicines at a
medical convention. A mythic family projected electronically

into a household seeking, at that moment, its own mythic and paradigmatic optimum as a family, is a natural for a cool sale. The soft pitch is the shoe-in.

There is a frightening corollary to this new stiff and iconic family whose male head addresses the nation as "we." George Orwell's novel *1984* paints the picture of a small ruling class, dominated by a savage puritan and Manichean ethic, that forbids itself the pleasures of sexual intercourse. Sex is believed to be deeply offensive to the collectivity proper to political action. The ruling class, however, permits and encourages every kind of license in the plebians in order to keep them from thinking about things non-biological.

The double standard between sexual abstinence in the ruling class and total permissiveness in the ruled today commences to work itself out of literature and into history. Senator Packwood of Oregon, a paterfamilias of high principle and marital rectitude, today urges a federal abortion bill upon Congress. Such men --dozens like him stare down the television glare-- would never permit their wives to sign a *New York Times* advertisement under the heading "I have had an abortion!" It would ruin them politically. But their espousal of abortion *for other people* forwards them politically.

The double standard --high old-fashioned standards for us aristocrats; anything for you, the plebians-- fingers the enormous differences between telepolitical imagery --Jungian familial completion-- and existence out on the streets. The United States, even before it faces the Packwood proposals, has already moved into a double standard of morality created by the coupling of reality bewitched into new being by television.

Even criminals cry when they see evil triumph on the tube.

11 The Telepolitical Collective Unconscious

Telepolitics is demonstrating the power of the Jungian archetypal, of the Platonic paradigmatic, over the radical relativism and permissiveness dominating our culture in its non-political life.

Drugs are extolled by youth; Hollywood parties end in the tragedy of five persons murdered; the academic establishment can preach fierce individualism in sexual morality; periodical journals scream the death of absolutes --all of this not only can be. It is.

Simultaneously, at the apex of corporate existence, emerges a new ethic which could prove savagely puritan. The simultaneity of Telepolitics has brought back into the public order the universally human archetype of the family. The family returns unsponsored by the churches. The return bursts out of something psychologically universal.

Within media, men today live universally. Electronic technology is the objective correlative of the Jungian collective unconscious, rendered obsolete by television. The political order is a glare whose content is again familial. It has to be. The clan is an extension of family. Once defined by its localism, the clan encompassed a Sicilian boy aiding mama and papa against tax collectors from Naples. Today clans are everywhere in the U.S.A. An ancient but universal human structure returns and it challenges older political categories. Everybody identifies with *The Godfather.*

There is a contrapuntal movement in television which reflects the relationship Gestalt psychology discovers in figure-ground interfacing. When the ground has been pulled out from underneath a cultural structure or a network of institutions, when a new ground begins to create its own institutions and begins to be created by them, the old *figure* --as Marshall McLuhan insists-- returns as symbol.

At this moment in the United States, the ground has been pulled out from underneath the monogamous family. The breakdown of the family, the institutionalization of widespread divorce, the disaffection of youth, the new conviction that parents do not "own" their children, the re-defining of male and female roles, the burgeoning of the communal family --all these have caused the old-fashioned archetypal family to return with a vengeance as a telepolitical symbol.

A reverse figure-ground situation exists in Canada. In Canada the family remains figure to a ground which is deeply conservative in both the English and French-speaking population. The swinger in Canada has no existential ground. Therefore, he is symbol, a throwback from a Regency or Bourbonic past. Thus television took an unknown university professor who was not even a politican and skyrocketed him to Prime Minister in less than three years. His brilliant image rested on his *not* being a family man. More profoundly, he gave off the image of a smart dresser, a sophisticate who could date Barbra Streisand one day and "a sweet young thing" the next, who insisted that his very public life remain private, who could associate with a playgirl in London during a Commonwealth conference and insist that it was nobody's business, even after the "lady" went on TV to brag about her VIP date. Canadians, fed up with their own conventionality, wanted to identify with that image --and were very disappointed when their swinging, kissing Prime Minister married conventionally and conservatively and became a father like everybody else.

Expo '67 had begun the desire for a change of image. Trudeau followed. In his brief year as Minister of Justice, his "daring" image -- to be later radiated electronically by television which made his facial expressions, his mannerisms and his famous shrug positively hypnotic to viewers-- began when he got rid of a law that made homosexuality a crime. He stated that the Government had no right to be in the bedrooms of the nation. This meant, of course, that the entire nation was in *his* bedroom.

149

Television always projects archetypically that which we have lost or never had. This stylization permits a people to live mythically.

Television is the most potent technology in the history of man to effect mythological participation in what we are not.

The telepolitical theater without reflects, in the United States, an unspoken theater within: man without woman is incomplete; boy without father isn't quite boy; girl from nowhere is suspect. These attitudes could have been conclusions of the older Christian ethic. Today they are electronic projections of a drama which plays out its theater within the common structure of the human psyche. The family has not returned in the United States on moral grounds. The family has returned simply because the subconscious has been externalized electronically.

12 The End of Ideology

Telepolitics coincides with the death of ideology.

Ideologies were born with literate culture. Men ideate principles they have read about; they hunt for individual instances falling under their universals; they apply them --thus the politics of the Procrustean bed. Ideology is an attempt to make historical man conform to an idealized social and political order. Ideology involves the ability to conceive an earthly paradise and then to project and predict the paradise forward in time. Ideologizing links beautifully with the principles governing mass production: conceive the Ford and then make it be. Socialism, Communism, the myriad varieties of early Fascism, and all the vague melioristic progressivisms are instances of ideology.

Ideological thinking, therefore, depends on the following: (1) The mind must be able to conceive the dream; (2) dream the dream; (3) execute it. Ideologues are always bookmen with a strong visual bias. Their pattern, dreamed by them through the eyes of the spirit, promises salvation just on the other side of the farther hills of history.

An ideology, as Yves Simon has pointed out, * is not a purely descriptive analysis of an historical situation which points to a concrete cure for whatever evils are found to exist therein; nor is an ideology a philosophy in the sense of a reasoned body of doctrine presumed to transcend the idiosyncrasies of the present historical moment. An ideology mingles philosophical pretensions with empirical description.

Marxism pretends to be an exact science of society, but it is only a science based upon a generalization of the concrete socio-economic situation of the nineteenth century. Marxism surmounted its first great crisis when Marxist predictions concerning the coming revolution of the proletariat were contradicted by history. The revolution broke out in agricultural Russia, not in industrial Germany or England. Lenin surmounted this first crisis in Marxist thought with his theory of Imperialism: capitalist powers would eat each other alive in their rush for colonies: their exhaustion would produce the revolution promised by Marx and Engels.

But there is nothing in Marxist theory capable of confronting a telepolitical world in which ideological expectation gives way to an electronic presence effectively canceling any rational movement from here to there or from today to tomorrow. This critique must not be read as predicting a failure for Communists. They mask the failure of classical Marxism by concentrating on existing injustices and poverty and wars everywhere outside their own empire. Blaming the existing capitalist order has been both effective and easy.

*The Tradition of Natural Law (New York: Fordham University Press, 1967)

A strong case can be made that Communists outside the
Iron Curtain have successfully bent television to their own
ends by imaging into existence a world of grief and war
which only waits on the healing hand of a new kind of
socialism. The success of this tactic is evidenced in the
obvious contradiction of "nationalist" or "separatist"
movements in Quebec, Ireland, and elsewhere, all embrac-
ing the socialist creed. This creed, of course, would wipe
these new "nations" --created anew by television-- off the
face of a Communist map that knows no such differentia
tion.

The issue is evidenced by the difference between the older
official Irish Republican Army and the new "Provisionals,"
the former pretentiously Marxist, the latter purely tribal and
sectarianly Catholic. Communism's failure to develop the
new media from within its own vast empire, to give its
practitioners --many of them highly talented-- free reign,
indicates the savage irony of an internal failure overcome
by an external success.

In a word: television monstrates problems crying out for
solution. Television's sensuous texture precludes the
abstract demonstration of dialectical materialism. Television
never promises distant goods, as Communism does. Television
delivers the goods even before they are promised.

Ambivalently hovering between an old world to be saved by
conventional mechanical industrialization and a new world
to be created, Marxism can successfully use television *only*
when it hides its own origins in literary culture, only when
it avoids the patent seriousness of culture as theater, as
play. Semi-literate Cuba is dominated by the master of them
all, the first TV actor in the world, Fidel Castro. But Castro
gives something far better than Germanic dialectical
promises: he gives Cuba a show!

To the degree to which television does not report but creates
its own world of images, television wraps man in this new

152

order which is internally oblivious to the older reality which ideology proposes to reform.

Cutting both ways, television is revealed as an enemy of ideology in all forms.

The twentieth century in the United States has been marked by the mingling of an older pragmatic politics and ideological dreaming. In the Roosevelt era old-fashioned pragmatism mixed with messianism. Taking care of the boys down in the precinct was confounded with taking care of the world.

America voted on the national level ideologically for the last time in 1964. Everyone knew what Barry Goldwater stood for because he told everybody what he believed. Goldwater was incapable of trimming his sails. In Tennessee he came out for the abolition of the TVA! His flirtation with military strategy in Vietnam confirmed him as a fanatical hawk, even before the dove-hawk terminology was current. Senator Goldwater's ideology was minimal but it was marked by a conviction that his nation ought to be a certain kind of America, visualized forward as a projection of what America had been in the last century. Ideologues are often painfully honest and, like all painfully honest men, they are terribly vulnerable. Lyndon Johnson's massive victory ended ideology in American politics for our time.

The first year of President Nixon's administration demonstrated all the more the bankruptcy of ideology.

He made his name as a furious anti-Communist; he was enthusiastically received in Bucharest for being the first American president to visit a Communist nation.

He thundered in the past against the welfare state; his welfare proposals have staggered the imagination of his most bitter critics from within the liberal establishment.

153

He stood for the free market; he scuttled it in one dramatic gesture in defense of the dollar.

Hawks swept him into power and he presented himself as Dove in his sweep across Asia.

He astounded the entire world by going to Red China in an effort at achieving a Washington-Peking rapprochement.

The issue has nothing to do with any supposed change in the soul of President Nixon. Sea changes involve a shift from one ultimate vision of the good life to its contradictory; this has not happened to Mr. Nixon. Once in power the President of the United States, the lord of the free world, was confronted with a kaleidoscope of problems crying for solutions.

But a problem for the President of the United States has nothing to do with ideology. Poor folk needing aid would remain precisely what they are under the boldest Fascism or the most fanatical Communism. Racial tension would be politically intolerable in any social order from that of Charlemagne to Charles de Gaulle. Hurricanes destroy towns, kill people. and leave in their wake misery and desolation. None of this is very ideological.

Conservatives and liberals, Communists and Fascists, Blacks and whites, beards and crew-cuts, given power, would have to make their work of mercy a corporate political act. The fanatics in our midst exist on the periphery of political life. Ideology today is at home only among them.

Disillusion with ideology permits one of two reactions: man can fall back either on an older ethic or act viscerally. Ironically enough, if we abstract from the sexual order, the visceral reaction almost always coincides with the older ethic.

Towns destroyed by hurricanes need outside aid; intellectually deficient children need a special kind of education; ghetto man needs gardens; smog and stuff must go; everybody is against muscular dystrophy and nobody likes cancer.

Telepolitics beams these issues into every home in the nation but Telepolitics does not do so without having first happened upon a certain hierarchy. With the decay of ideology even behind the Iron Curtain, the hierarchy increasingly becomes a set of priorities in which men place to the forefront what they consider to be important and relegate to a back seat what they consider to be unimportant. Men in power commence to philosophize about good and evil, even in the teeth of the dominant liberalism. What happens in between good and evil forms a sliding scale.

To summarize:

A hidden TV war is the war between totalitarian questions, dictated by older ideologies, and the newer hierarchy of human questions demanding immediate solution by a medium impatient with ideologies and innocent of time, of the future, of "putting off" today what can only be done tomorrow.

13 The Brief Eden of Privacy

Hobbe's jungle theory suggests that we are first in the jungle and then leave it in order to emerge into civilization. The linear bias of early modernity could not be more patent. Rousseau is full of the same sort of thing. First we are in an idyllic, pastoral, natural world and then we leave it for the evils of society. First we are savages, noble or ignoble. Then we are members of society, good or evil. Is it not true, however, that we structure our past in the light of our future and that we remember what we do and as we do only because of where we are going, or where we think we are going?

155

Heidegger phenomenologized this insight which is as old as St. Augustine's break with the classical understanding of history as a cycle.

"Anthropology deals with the future of the past, but historical thinking involves the future of the past together with the past of the future." *

The future of Hobbes' jungle will be the past of contemporary civilization. Both civility and savagery mingle together in a kind of harmonic opposition. Nowhere is this more evident than in man's corporate --that is to say, political-- attitude towards privacy.

John Lukacs points out that privacy was an invention of the modern age, an inheritance of the bourgeois spirit. The young do not miss privacy; they have never known privacy. They are puzzled by those of their elders who still insist upon this bizarre stance in their lives. Children cannot understand why adults are appalled when they return from work to find their middle-class suburban homes crawling with bearded Vikings playing expensive stereos at screeching pitch, conversations mingling with necking, dancing with sprawling on the floor. The reaction of the adults is less moral than aesthetic. The momentary panic to flee this barbarism and simply to get away and be alone with one's self is a daily temptation to tens of millions of American fathers and mothers. The drop-out urge is not peculiar to the young.

Nonetheless, the very passion for privacy is nothing particularly adult in itself, nor is the passion to live in a communitarian and participatory rhythm something that is particularly endemic to the young. The very Nordic and Viking look of our bearded youth was once the commonplace visage of aged Norsemen and Danes. The very old usually slept in an enormous bed; middle and younger generations --men and

*John Lukacs, *Historical Consciousness* (New York: Harper & Row, 1968) p.16

women, children and graybeards-- huddled together against the cold in one huge room wherein were performed not only the rites of love, but the necessities of the body as well. Tribesmen young and old lived together.

Even when this residual savagery was conquered in the Middle Ages, there emerged no equivalent of the modern "interior life" or "private stance." Sin was something done publicly and punished publicly, as violent as the murder of Thomas à Becket and the corporate flogging of King Henry II. The "presence of God" was not the imaginatively reconstructed Calvary forged within the spirit by a Jesuit retreat master in the age of the High Baroque. "The presence of God" was the physical Christ in the tabernacle, the *Sacramentum:* The Thing!

Politics had nothing to do with ideas. Politics was the gay livery a man wore when he went out to battle. Coats of arms took the place of issues and ideologies. Politics was as bloody and physical and personal as was religion. The discovery of an interior dimension, of an imagined space, of a private garden within the heart of man, was a peculiarly modern addition to the human experience. Prefigured by the ideals of earlier contemplative orders of religion, the ideal was secularized and made available to anyone who could aspire to the bourgeois style of life.

Dominating the modern era, most especially in its later periods, the very possibility of achieving privacy was identified with success.

And with privacy came guilt as a permanent human condition. Expiation for "sin" can be burned out of a man once and for all if he lives publicly. A whipping pays for the theft of a hen. But the interiorization of the consciousness --we might also call it the discovery of consciousness-- involved as well the interiorization of guilt and the impossibility of public expiation. Freudianism has been one long and ambitious attempt to re-exteriorize guilt.

157

But Freudianism is obsolete today because electric
families have exteriorized consciousness. Does the new
electronic clan involve a necessary destruction of privacy?
The issue cannot be answered in any linear fashion which
would suggest that the public life yielded to the private and
that the private now yields again to the public.

In our age of the total presence of all historic ideals to all
men everywhere, the situation has been rendered enormously
ambiguous. The global village has personalized industrial
man but it has done so in such a fashion that he keenly
remembers the recent past when he was not personal at all.
Anonymity has become a dream for him. The escape from
wife and children, from business and church, is projected
mythologically into a kind of liberation in which he roams
megalopolis, well-heeled, altogether unknown, therefore free.

Whereas privacy was a necessary component of our
immediate past, privacy today has returned as a symbolic
figure that floats in the air altogether without any proper
ground of its own. The flight from the cities to the suburbs was a frantic search for a privacy fading before the
march of monolithic mechanization. The spawning of
private clubs and private schools, the hot-house existence
of high society in the United States with its "coming-out"
rites and its debutante balls, its rigid social code, its
Byzantine rituals as to who could enter and who could not,
all marked the principled insistence of monied Americans
that they would be private. But this very thirst for privacy,
involving --as it did-- fencing an entire class away from
the broad body of the polity, undid what it set out to do.
Instead of finding privacy, the American upper class
mechanized itself in the most savage ways. Today many of
these same rich Americans find privacy by fleeing back into
the anonymity of the inner city, in social work, in religion,
in weekend sprees.

But what is anonymity for suburbia is corporate life for the
inner city. Are we, perhaps, commencing to live in a time

when private and communitarian life are interfaces? when
one man's privacy is another man's communal life? when
"dropping-out" truly means "dropping-in"?

If every historical age today, thanks to the new technology,
is a presence and if every historical ideal is a real possibility,
then it would seem to follow that nothing any longer can
be accepted as the definitive negation of anything else. We
do not refer, of course, to principled acceptance of one
doctrine over other doctrines. The fundamental law of the
mind remains that of non-contradiction; i.e., no two positions
can be entertained simultaneously and in the same way by
one man at any one moment of time and in any one act of
judgment.

We refer, rather, to options concerning ways of being, ways
of living, styles of life. As interfacing tensions, *all* are
present to late twentieth century man.

This is not only true of the "private" and "public" man,
of Kissinger being seen in Washington night clubs and Nixon
not being seen at all and Howard Hughes being seen and
not seen everywhere. "Private" and "public" are, after
all, matters of preference.

The simultaneous possibility of all possibilities in the electric
age marks, for our time, the impossibility of stamping the
immediate future with any recognizable life style, with any
motif or public orthodoxy that could possibly transcend this
or that electronic kinship. Even more, although the new
and old kinships sustained electronically maintain a kind
of internal consistency as political units, men generally belong to, or can move within, more than one neuron. They
manifest an ambiguity not found in older tribes. In an
age of the mask, electronic man slips from ball to ball as
from masquerade to masquerade.

There are our Julian Bonds who play both the establishment
Democratic game with one hand and the Black Power game

159

with the other. Even more: there are men who sense themselves as belonging to only one neuron, but who can move
around freely in any number of neurons. They both con-
firm and contravene David Riesman's sociology of the fifties.
Riesman spoke of men with no convictions who had their
radar antennas out for everyone else in order to gain acceptance. Today we have millions with conviction who can fake
it nonetheless with hostile clans. The mask dominates everywhere, with or without internal conviction.

Plato's wisdom tells us that we are never going to get a
society dominated by wise men. Even if we did, Plato
suggests wryly, we (or our wives) would not like it anyhow.
Every cultural epoch hitherto has been dominated by a type
which has been formed in the likeness of an ideal: i.e., martial honor, material wealth, liberty, full expression of the
passions. Granted that all these goals mingle together in
most men and therefore can be found everywhere at all
times, Plato's insight governing the dominance of one over
the others has been verified (roughly verified: history permits
of nothing more) periodically in time.

This kind of succession is prohibited us today due to electronic simultaneity. The heroic chivalry of timocracy mingles
with the acquisitiveness of capitalist man; the open liberty
of democracy exists side by side with the dark voluptuousness
of tyranny. In a sense the *form* of democracy conquers even
as the content of democracy withers into one among a
number of alternatives facing post-modern man.

There is scarcely a reader of this book who has not girded
himself with Quixote against the windmills; who has not
bent himself to the task of pursuing riches with Locke;
who has not sensed with relief the dawn of liberty with
Thomas Paine; who has not been massaged into delight
and despair by the permissiveness of the age. Just as private
and public are no longer alternatives for contemporary man
because both are realities, so too, past civilizational styles
are not alternative futures because they are already present.

160

Part III
Democracies before and after Television

1 The Nature of American Democracy

The United States of America historically has gloried in being pragmatically indifferent to philosophy and has justified this conviction by lifting pragmatism itself to the status of being "The American Philosophy."

Thomas Paine's exaltation of the French Revolutionary Rights of Man swept like a brush fire through the colonies in the years immediately preceding the Revolution. But Paine's proselytizing atheism and his rationalism were offensive to a basically Christian and conservative people.

The young Republic looked not to philosophy but to law. No society in late modern times has had a richer development in law and a finer body of written meditation on its own jurisprudence.

The American Revolution and the institutions which grew out of it were the work of men influenced around the edges by the idealism of Rousseau, but firmly rooted in the older classical tradition.

The new Republic initially was not supposed to be an ideological projection of all dreams of the human heart, but a limited government whose modest goal was to guarantee the rights of its citizenry.

The ideological fever within the American experience was introduced only much later with the abolitionist movement.

The Battle Hymn of the Republic was the exultant song of the nation at arms that considered itself to be a new Jerusalem, the sword of the vengeance of God. Religious messianism thus mingled with older and more modest classical norms. The rash of self-interpretation that swept both the North and the South in the years preceding the Civil War was extinguished with the definitive victory of the Union over the Confederacy.

In this century American intellectuals have only recently turned to the philosophical explanation of their own experience, and they have done so at the precise moment when that experience is being called into question everywhere.

The United States today is producing its political philosophers; in so doing, the United States would seem to be following the curve of history. We have all gone to "look for America," in the words of the popular song.

The late political philosopher Willmoore Kendall and Professor Martin Diamond have emphasized that the American Constitution was explicated rationally and definitively by the *Federalist Papers.*

Running through that hydra-authored document is the fear that some day, sooner or later, a faction would threaten the domestic peace and smooth ordering of a hard-working society bent on the acquisition of wealth. (Diamond)

Factions put convictions, especially religious convictions, higher in their priority of goods than the pursuit of money, and other riches. Factions are peopled by men hell-bent for

162

heaven on earth. They disturb artisans and farmers and other godly folk more interested in tilling the soil, expanding commerce, and raising their children into inheritances hard come by.

The very pathology of the faction is its ability to raise the political temperature of the nation, agitate passions better kept dormant, and thus create a temporary majority (Kendall) burning with zeal for the legalizing and enforcing of this or that popular cause.

Abolition, free silver, and the civil rights movement have been the most significant factions within American political history. All three succeeded in converting themselves with varying degrees of success into the warp and woof of the American public orthodoxy.

Electronic decentralization has turned every neuronic group into a faction.

These electronic factions, however, cannot work their message into a nation which has lost the older homogeneity which rendered agreement possible.

2 Cabdriver Democracy

A *temporary* majority creates what Yves Simon*--himself a Frenchman turned American, a cautious friend of the French Revolution and a convinced friend of the American-- called the "cabdriver theory of democracy."

The elected representatives of the people are the voice of what the people want here-and-now-in-this-very-moment for which the people send their representatives to the nation's capital. The perfection of this type of democracy, we add, is democracy by plebiscite or referendum.

*Philosophy of Democratic Government, (Chicago; University of Chicago Press, 1951).

163

Such democracy, nurtured in the nineteenth and come to fruition in the twentieth century, finds its perfection in the leader who asks the citizens to vote and ratify his policies, to indicate a national confidence in his being the political stethoscope of the heart of the people. This was the tactic used effectively by Napoleon III in his rise to power. His assumption of the imperial title was merely ratified once he had already gained power. But it was precisely this set of circumstances that *The Federalist,* interpreting the Constitution, attempted to avoid.

The Bastille and the guillotine were totally foreign to a new nation of farmers and artisans and shipbuilders. We had no Parisian mob crying for bread and blood in the name of a Platonic heaven of abstract "Rights of Man."

The young Republic, in the words of Calvin Coolidge, wanted to get about the business of America: business. The early American opponents of cabdriver democracy, the authors of the *Papers*, as interpreted by their latter day commentators in any event, flashed out their original objection. Not only does commitment to causes get in the way of acquisition of material goods but this kind of democracy is ephemeral. Mesmerized into the streets and town-halls of the nation out of the drifting clouds of men haunted by dreams of perfection, a mob will not want tomorrow what it wants today.

Nothing is more transitory than the applause of the street.

The Parisian mob applauded King Louis XVI and then killed him. The horror of the French experience was always before the eyes of the early American Republic. Democracy --in the French sense of the term-- was as abominable as was the British Crown. Cabdriver democracy suffers the fate of all cabdrivers. The fare gets off when he wants to. Danton was the hero of the day. He was executed by Robespierre. Robespierre was then executed by the moderates. Without

Napoleon, the macabre movie would have never been brought to a halt.

Contemporary American analysts of our history such as Diamond and Kendall are agreed substantively that a radically politicized order heats people up beyond their capacities to function in nonpolitical ways. This tends to bring to a halt the politically cooling tendency that goes with men and families whose priorities are personal economic success and not political adventuring.

The entire sweep of American history can be read in terms of a successful attempt to keep the enthusiasts down and the system going. The abolitionist movement and the bloody Civil War were tragic exceptions.

3 Democratic Consensus

The political genius of democracy by consensus resided in its keen awareness that time heals everything, both the zeal of the New as well as the zeal of the Old. The symbiosis of old and new was presumed to be a kind of catalyst which defined the genius of the American experience; liberalism converting itself into conservatism and conservatism into liberalism. Time was supposed to soften the harshness of the absolute. Historic Europe never understood this unique political compromise.

Consensus, as Kendall and others have argued, means acceptance of change by an initially reluctant minority. This minority is convinced by an initally enthusiastic majority subsequently mellowed by time.

Any "movement" seeking radical change --so goes the theory-- had to expose itself to a series of legislative roadblocks and judicial decisions which take time, much time. Initial emotional commitments are cooled off. This weakens numerically the proponents of revolutionary change. Simultaneously, this cooling produced by time and the sheer

165

need to submit proposals to the "democratic process" gives a minority opposed to sharp changes the time needed to adjust to a new situation.

Time --gained by institutions that insist that nothing happen precipitously and that look with imperious contempt upon artificially contrived pressures-- both tempers adherents of, and softens opponents to, the New.

Irish independence is an ideal as old as the Pale of Dublin, England's first beachhead on the Emerald Isle, and this happened five hundred years ago.

Democracy by consensus can exist only when men disagree, no matter how deep their disagreements might be, on means which are absorbed within larger ends, themselves constituting the public orthodoxy or consensus of society. The ideological nature of European parties makes it impossible for them to accept on any grounds stronger than the pure mechanics of government, the dominance of another ideological faction. Time does not soften the harshness of the absolute in Continental Europe.

The United States insisted that government by the people was not to be understood in terms of what fifty-one percent of the electorate wants right now. A constitutional majority means a consensus by a majority that has reconciled the minority and proven its toughness by enduring.

4 The Dwindling Majority

Today the ephemeral majority feared by the Federalist can only be created out of the dwindling majority, soon to become a minority, of citizens constituting Middle America. They consider themselves to be citizens first and believers in this or that religion or absolute second.

Majorities, when created by the power of media, tend to evaporate with the very rapidity with which they were

166

fashioned. Enthusiasms for causes can be bewitched into being on television, but they fade even more swiftly than did the temporary majorities in the past. Television has the power to mobilize opinion in a broad spectrum of the population and to do so rapidly. This power is antithetical to television's decentralizing and discontinuous dynamism. Discontinuous grouping, therefore, cancels out the possibility of mobilizing a "nation in arms" marching like one man to the tune of the Will of the People. There are simply too many non-spatial "peoples" or "nations" today.

Both French and American type democracies demand a national state created by print technology and governed from a centralized zone of power through a vast bureaucracy that passes down orders and spreads them uniformly through a limited space bounded by frontiers.

Television replaces print by the audiotactile.

Television splinters the homogeneous nation into discontinuous and self-containing units. Television curtails the middleman of bureaucracy by eliminating the need to transmit messages from here to there through messengers, middlemen.

Television renders frontiers irrelevant.

5 The Democracy of the Dead

Consensus is a peculiarly American way of controlling the "hot heads." In Europe and South America the brakes have been in nondemocratic institutions, the monarchy in England, the church and the army in Europe and Latin America.

Rousseau's "general will" demands that what the majority wants right now, it gets right now. But for more than two hundred years this kind of democracy has been opposed by institutions which presumably enshrine traditions and heritages which transcend the passions of the street. Minorities, often small but more often large, claimed to stand for the historic essence of the nation against the democratic mob.

Since these traditionalists could never hope to win at the polls they reposed their authority in either the church or the army, custodians of a tradition thought to be bigger than the majoritarian instincts and convictions of the democrats. Carlists in Spain and Legitimists in France; *caudillos* riding out of the vast pampa in Argentina; military juntas from Paraguay to Athens; all based their claim to power not on majority rule but on the sense of history they claimed to incarnate, i.e., on "the democracy of the dead," Chesterton's famous definition of tradition.

6 Time and American Democracy

The basic political instability in the Latin world since the French Revolution has been caused by the dual between democracy and tradition.

The opposition dialectic was blurred deliberately in the United States by checks and balances.

Ultimate power was thought to reside in the Congress, which mirrored, most especially in the House of Representatives, the immediate preoccupations and convictions of a majority of voting citizens given the franchise.

The six-year term given senators was designed less to represent the States than to cool down the heat of the House. A man with six years in office is not as dependent on the whims of his constituency as is a man who must stand for re-election every two years.

Relative independence from the will of a constituency permits a politician to exercise his own judgment.

The four-year term given the President attempted to strike a monarchical balance between the relative aristocracy of the Senate and the relative democracy of the House.

The federal courts, most especially the Supreme Court, were removed from any pressures that derived from a transient majority or dominant faction.

The genius of the system is grasped when we penetrate its understanding of *time* as a factor in political existence.

If a "movement" --such as abolition, free silver, or civil rights-- wanted to make its cause part and parcel of the law of the land, it had to gain the acquiescence of the majority. And this takes time, a time-taking built into the very judicial structure of the Constitution.

Our question: how has Telepolitics altered this traditionalist interpretation of American democracy?

7 Instant Democracy

Telepolitics cancels time-taking because natural time is annihilated within electronics.

Total cabdriver democracy looks like a possibility. Men could today "cast their vote" instantaneously and simultaneously on any and every political issue. All he need do is push buttons. All Telepolitics need do is provide the buttons to execute the will of the majority. But this will of the majority would be what the majority wanted *at that moment.*

However, government by electronic majority is possible only if there exist an electronic majority. We believe the decentralizing effects of electronics render national majorities not only ephemeral but obsolescent. Neuronic Man is non-majoritarian.

Earlier, the telephone and the telegraph eliminated time-taking in message-sending. The decline in letter-writing, slowed down because letters are cheap, attests to a world that will not write messages and then entrust them to the post office when long-distance phone calls will do the job instantaneously.

Video-phones will simply hasten a process already begun a century ago. Cradled in electronic simultaneity, the generations bred on TV are impatient, as indicated, for immediate solutions to problems immediately beamed into the living room.

Everyone senses that the elaborate and lengthy time sequences that are part and parcel of American legality --appeals, court processes, amendments to national and state constitutions, referral to committees, etc.-- are a kind of shadowy movie in slow motion that no longer corresponds to political reality.

The new media do not permit traditional reflection any more than the slowly considered answer which weighs all alternatives can compete with the fast quip on the *Today* show. Nowhere is this more evident than in the President's *de facto* power to wage war in Korea or Vietnam without war having been declared *de jure* by the Congress.

In the world in which the hot-line between the Kremlin and the White House exists in order to prevent an accidental war because of some human flaw in our frightening technology, the constitutional duty to debate the issue of war or peace on a global scale has been rendered obsolete.

Castro's Cuba is counterpoint to the United States in the game of Telepolitics.

Cuba, along with all South America, has no tradition of uninterrupted constitutionalism. The history of Latin America could be written in terms of the substitution of one paper

170

constitution for another. The artificial dominance of the
written word in basically oral cultures has been a significant
cause of political instability south of the Rio Grande. South
American society has been able to endure a game of political
musical chairs in which one government replaces another in
bewildering, and eventually boring, sequence because of
deeper underlying institutions based on an oral and person-
alistic tradition.

The United States was created by print and therefore has
always sensed that a violation of the written constitution
would cause a national trauma. Whenever the Supreme Court
changed the Constitution in recent times, it did so in
the name of that very document. Abstract legality chiseled
into print is the very spine of the American experience.
In South America the overwhelming dominance of the family
with its consequent nepotism, linked with the church and
the army, formed a political order underneath the official
politics of the state. Castro can govern Cuba over television
and can issue ukase after ukase because he is not burdened
by an Anglo-Saxon political tradition.

8 Ant-Heap Democracy

Television is presumed to be able to centralize and create a
monolithic culture.

Such a presumption reveals a profound misunderstanding of
electronic effects. Only someone who blurred the distinction
between mechanical and electronic technology, could project the monolithic and egalitarian characteristics of the
former onto the latter. This complaint simply extends to
electronic technology the same criticism it launches against
the effects of mechanical technology. The theory goes that
mechanical order fragments society by breaking up older
and non-rationalized modes of production and life. This
shattered mechanical order, then, reintegrates by central-

171

izing hitherto autonomous units into larger economic and
social structures.

A society totally mechanized at the base and governed from
above electronically by a totalitarian elite would, of course,
produce an ant-heap civilization whose lineaments have been
traced for us in novels and movies. Such a civilization could
exist for only a precariously short moment in history because
electronics tend, by an inner dynamism, to decentralize and
thus to undo the effects of mechanization. This is precisely
the situation we encounter in the late twentieth century in
the most technologically advanced country in the world,
the United States of America.

As the authors have argued in *The War in Man,** contemporary American man is forced to live within two opposite
antithetical technological rhythms, the older mechanical
and newer electronic. The situation is painful but transit-
ional.

Conversely, electronics does not destroy an already existent
oral and non-rationalized society. The older ground, the
older media, now becomes the content of the newer electronic forms. Older forms become symbolic figures: swords hang
on walls; cable cars decorate gardens; river boats become
restaurants. These symbolic figures are tolerated and even
encouraged as play, but they are crushed when they dare to
challenge the newer technologies that have replaced them
as work.

In the movie, *The Vanishing Point,* the last mechanical man,
a washed-out racing driver, hopped up on speed, makes a mad
dash in a souped-up 1970 Dodge Charger, not in the Indianapolis 500, but across the country on public roads. His
heroic ride against inevitable failure, truly in the grand
tradition, is charted by police radar screens that envelop

*Frederick Wilhelmsen and Jane Bret, *The War in Man: Media and
Machines,* (Athens, Georgia: Georgia University Press, 1970)

172

him in their electronic womb as effectively as igloos cover
an Eskimo family or cages fence in mating rabbits. Our
sympathies are with the driver because the odds are overwhelmingly against him. His flaming death on the road
was high tragedy. Is this the mechanical robot as nostalgic
hero?

Robot civilization is not ahead of us; it is behind us. By a
curious trick of the imagination we tend to project into the
future the horrors of the present or the immediate past. We
do so, presumably, in order to make the misery of time
present more tolerable by advancing the date of the calendar
of history.

When men are within an evolutionary situation, predictions
about the future are possible in varying degrees of accuracy.
The body structure of a three-year-old child permits its
parents to make a reasonably accurate guess as to how the
child will look at the age of six. Past performance in one area
is a reasonable criteria for projecting future performance
within the same area.

Predictions, therefore, about an unfolding technology can
be made within the suppositions of that very technology.
The humanist predictions of a gray beehive existence are
as old as Samuel Butler's attack against machine technology
in the nineteenth century. They were later advanced by
William Morris and the Pre-Raphaelites. They became the
stock-in-trade of Chesterton and Belloc's Distributist
Movement in England and of the Southern Agrarians in
their manifesto, "I'll Take My Stand."

More recently similar critiques were advanced by Juenger
in Germany and Marcel in France. Projecting an existent
movement towards uniformity into the future, these men
accurately predicted what the future would have been were
it to have been mechanical. They failed to note that the new
electronic technology was based on principles antithetical to
those operative within mechanics. Therefore its effects are

173

not deducible from the mechanized cultures of the nineteenth and early twentieth centuries.

9 The Electronic Jungle

An anarchical and chaotic jungle of competing neuronic
loyalties does not threaten to make real Chesterton's fantasy,
The Napoleon of Notting Hill, in which a London suburb
declares its independence and wages war against England. The
fantasy is already reality. Those who accept internally as an
ultimate authority in politics the old absolutes of the national state are a dwindling majority that clings to middle-class
cultural patterns, that drops back into them after a tribal
spree, or that still lives by the old American dream of
rising from rags to riches. Middle America --the America
of Spiro Agnew *and* of his respectable liberal critics-- is
still a working majority within the United States. But this
majority is shrinking daily.

Revolutionary political action --propounded by Weathermen,
Yippies, S.D.S., Black Power and others-- whose concrete
tactics shift from day to day and reach all existing institutions from church to university to prison, simply does not
accept the premises of "the System." Even those tens of
millions on the Right who wrap themselves in the flag and
who recall a past glory will continue to accept "the System"
only so long as it retains sufficient substantive content
inherited from the forefathers.

Should "the System" prove so elastic out of an intelligent
insight into its own weakness that it embraces too many
revolutionary causes and thus legitimizes them, the Right
wing --as we have indicated-- will become the largest tribe
in America, while abominating the Establishment with the
same venom found in the Berrigan brothers.

174

The Praetorians --Are they coming?

The tramping feet of the Praetorians to the drums of counter-revolution is no distant threat to American order. The Praetorians are already armed and show themselves restless under the command of an Establishment that to them seems too weak to move. When the police of America have their own channel or channels, a new and powerful tribe of men who feel themselves abused daily by the going media will spring into history and no man will then know who is hunted and who is hunter, who is draped in the mantle of law and who is not. The lawman of the movie *Dirty Harry* may very well be a new American hero.

10 Tolerance as a Political Category

The genius of the classical American political tradition re-vealed an understanding of the virtue of tolerance rarely surpassed in history. Tolerance must not be confused with indifference. Men indifferent to issues are outside the theater of debate. They simply don't care. This withdrawal from judgment is often confused with tolerance because both involve a "hands off" or *laissez-faire* style of life. Tolerance, unlike indifference, means to put up with a person or situation which is abrasive to one's convictions in a sliding scale of intensity. The man of deep religious con-viction may put up with views which he considers to be heretical; so does the man of less intense religious conviction. The tolerance of the first is greater than that of the second because the irritant is stronger.

The same situation exists in the political order. But this formal consideration is incomplete unless linked to psycho-logy. What is monstrous and totally intolerable when first encountered is rendered more tolerable with increasing familiarity. Dr. Samuel Johnson abominated transgressions against the moral order from out of the depths of his High Church Anglican orthodoxy, but he was at ease in the company of whores because of his years spent in poverty

175

as a journalist who rubbed shoulders with the demi-monde. Tolerance does not preclude friendship with the man whose views or behavior is tolerated although tolerance does not demand friendship.

The issue is of significance in this context because majority and minority, when grouped about a "cause," are never initially tolerant of one another. The ascetic discipline, forced on a new majority (itself a minority yesterday) espousing a "cause," of making its movement the law of the land, demanded that it talk to the recalcitrant conservative minority. In talking to the minority and in subjecting itself to the legislative and judicial processes institutionalized in the American Constitution, the majority grew tolerant of the minority by simply playing the same game with it.

The minority, yesterday the majority, is not forced to simply surrender to the fifty-one percent of the electorate on issues affecting constitutional changes which promise to alter the fabric of society. The minority can soften the harshness of the new by attaching riders to proposed legislation or by delaying full and immediate implementation in the courts. These delaying tactics are used initially with the hope of defeating the new. Subsequently, the tactics are employed to stave off inevitable failure, the way in which medicine holds back death. But by entering into dialogue with the majority the minority educates itself in inevitability, once convinced that it cannot win. This education eases the pain. The radicalism of yesterday, intolerable and abominated, becomes the unpleasant irritant, disapproved of but tolerated today.

11 Tolerance as a Telepolitical Category

Television would seem to possess two antithetical tendencies so far as tolerance is concerned. As a formal structure calling forth a synthesis of sensorial and intellectual functions that involve the viewer in an act of participation, television does not produce tolerance at all. It is far more difficult to

176

tolerate a telephone call which takes us away from the television screen than it is to tolerate an interruption in our reading. We can pick up our magazine or book and continue with the passage we were reading when interrupted. But we cannot replay televised images which have punished us by destroying our participation for having left the tube for the phone. Television is similar to interruptions in conversation with the difference that our wills can re-direct conversation to where it was when we were called to the door or phone. Such re-direction (a possibility tomorrow, of course, because of cassette TV) has been impossible thus far.

Tolerance demands, of its very nature, that we pay attention to the man or situation tolerated. Total participation excludes paying attention to anything outside the context in question.

Tolerance, prejudice to the contrary, is not a cool stance; tolerance demands a high degree of heat, of tension in which anomalies and antinomies are juxtaposed and in which men live within that very juxtaposition. For this reason, tolerance tends to slide into indifferentism, into the "I don't care" syndrome. Indifferentism dissolves the tension.

The "heat" engendered by tolerating the undesired is "cooled off" not only by the tube but by the relaxing media of easy chairs and couches, cold beer and pretzels, darkened den or living room, family gathered not as parent ordering or child being ordered by him, not as wife and husband facing one another as sex partners or as business associates. This "coolness" cannot tolerate the intrusion of The Other: The Other annihilates in a split second the familial liturgy being enacted through the massaging of each participant by a nexus of media that work more effectively in proportion to their not being noticed at all. No actor on Broadway or singer for the Met can tolerate a noisy drunk in a conspicuous box seat, even if the content of the play or opera is an apoligia for tolerance itself.

177

If television *as a form* is intolerant, for example, of
hot personalities because they are not tolerant, the *content*
of television is totally indifferent to either tolerance or intolerance *as ideated substance.* Television's content is the
user, whether he be in the station or in the home receiving.
On both sides of the tube the medium is the message!

The ritualistic liberalism about the desirability of "tolerance"
understood as indifference to all absolutes except those
honed out of the liberal creed has been the abstract content
of most television since its inception. Television did not
create this content; television simply relayed it and spread it to
the world.

12 Telepolitics and Liberalism

Allen Drury's "Inside the White House - 1971" (*Look,*
October, 1971) rings up the customary charges against the
media's hostility to President Nixon and gives credence to
Vice President Agnew's celebrated attacks on both press and
television for their bias against all political figures thought to
be even a shade to the right of center. Although absolutely
true, the accusations fail to locate the bias in the all-englobing
liberalism that had become a public orthodoxy in America
for everybody except the revolutionary Left and the hardened
Right.

We have already suggested that the Establishment clips the
wings of the far Left when it turns its leaders into televised
personalities and we have noted that the staying power of
old veterans on the Right is often proportionate to their
having not been televised. But television's liberalism is the
consequence of that medium's capability of mirroring an
existing political and social phenomenon, and expanding it.
Yet television's deepest strength is not its power to report.

Television, as we have already mentioned, creates a new
reality. The media experts and consultants who fashion
candidates into images and who bewitch into existence tele-

political theater have already demonstrated their power to check the dominant liberalism. Mr. Nixon can take genuine pride that he has never knuckled under to media pressure but he must also remember that his own smooth media campaign made him President of the United States. The answer to a reflected and mirrored liberalism is not to be found in the appeals to "fair play" and "honesty" in reporting. Nor is the answer to be found in unseating the dominant liberalism back home outside the media. The shattering of the nation into autonomous classes has practically destroyed old-fashioned liberalism.

The answer is quite simply a media war against the media, the creation of a new electronic politics that does not stop with the victory of candidates and the dismantling, the day after election, of the smooth-running teams that made victory possible.

Truth is utterly irrelevant in Telepolitics if by "truth" we mean a matching of "reality." The "truth" of liberalism is already established as an ideological absolute which fashions colored spectacles through which the world is seen. Any hostile "truth" must do what liberalism has done: "seize the media and make its own being *be.*"

This is almost psychologically impossible for the American Right because of its inbuilt hostility to new forms of aesthetic existence. The chairman of the San Francisco State College Faculty of Broadcasting* lamented publicly that most of the students fed into radio and television broadcasting were liberals, but he defended himself on the grounds that these were practically the only young men and women who came to his school for an education in the media. This has nothing to do with democracy, but with preference.

* Dr. Stuart Hyde, Broadcast Preceptor Award Conference, San Francisco State, 1971.

Tolerance as indifference to non-liberal attitudes and convictions has been transmitted to a youth bred on TV. This youth largely mouths the slogans of an older liberal rhetoric that youth itself is replacing, because the Second American Revolution has not yet hammered out its own political symbolism. In fact, American youth today is savagely intolerant of whatever falls outside its own understanding of tolerance. The reaction of youth simply exemplifies the tribalization effected by electronic decentralization.

The reality will have gone out of democracy. A clan, by its very formal structure, demands the heat of internal tolerance. The smaller the clan, the more abrasive are its members to one another, the more garish and glaring appear individual faults, the more bitter are internal disputes. We need only think of the internal rancor marking all refugee or emigre movements.

The apparent internal intolerance --in reality, tolerance-- found in a clique of high school or college students borders on what theologians call a failure in charity. But so long as the clique or gang remains itself, its members tolerate one another against the "enemy" from outside.

Intolerance is another name for the divorce court. But this internal tolerance --a kind of love supporting hate for the sake of the common good-- is intolerant of whatever lies beyond itself as a possible or actual threat to its existence.

The tribal wars are being heated up and *very soon, with more than one hundred thousand transmitting stations in competition with each other --a safe prediction for the end of the decade-- democracy as we have known it will be a memory and possibly an empty symbol.*

13 Democracy, Law, Loyalty

Possibly every political order is democratic at bottom because nobody can govern, be he king or oligarch or party leader or assembly, without the consent of the governed. But democracy as we have known it in the Western tradition has meant the primacy of the law and the defense of the law by an overwhelming majority of citizens who split into pluralities and minorities over the content of the law but not the form. This sense of citizenship, as old as Greek democracy, subordinates familial and dynastic and even religious loyalties to the majesterial impersonality of the law: justice blindfolded and hence weighing the merits of any case in its court totally without reference to the persons involved.

Plato argued in *The Statesman* that government by law would be inferior to government by a wise man because incarnate wisdom could legislate in the concrete whereas the law can only command universally. Therefore the law occasionally sins against justice. Wisdom would judge each case on its merits; law must sweep all cases within its impersonal universality. But the same Plato taught that in fact no man is wise enough to be entrusted with this awesome responsibility and therefore government by laws is the best we can get on this earth.

What is not all that clear in Plato is the massive truth that all familial government, all tribal government, every arrangement of men into clans, is based on something deeper than law: loyalty. Now loyalty ultimately is given only to persons who are believed to be the repositories of the authority of the political group in question.

The modern paterfamilias who writes a constitution for the better governing of his family is simply funny. Rules, tacked on the kitchen wall, regulating the use of car and lawnmower, are made to be broken. The head of the family interprets these rules and his government over the family is ultimately personal. So-called familial "laws" are simply guide-posts for action. A rule is not a law: Aquinas saw this seven hundred years ago.

181

Ultimate decisions concerning right and wrong are determined personally. Historically in the West there has been
a synthesis between personal authority in government and
impersonal law. The synthesis worked reasonably well
because both personal and impersonal in politics were
kept in balance.

In the Middle Ages, the personalism of German tribalism did
not quite swamp the impersonality of Roman law   In early
modernity, the personalism of English Whiggery, oligarchy
rampant, did not quite swamp the impersonality of the
medieval common law. In late modernity, the impersonality
of democracy did not quite swamp the personalism of
familial autonomy.

14 Technology: East and West

No serious student of media denies that totally-involved
kinship groups are our immediate future. But it is an
immediate future because it is our present, that is to say,
our past. We constantly let the *third eye* glued in the back
of our heads take over the function of the two eyes with
which we look ahead.

An interesting contrast to this attitude can be found in
comparing Eastern and Western historical approaches to
technology. Whereas the West, due to its highly developed
sense of historical time understands the past as past, the
East has historically experienced the past as a mythic *now.*
The East historically rejected technology as a threat to the
primacy of this continuity of human experience. The
Western philosopher Hegel dismissed Eastern philosophy as
being identical with Eastern religion, and therefore no philosophy at all. From this point of view the East held all
technologies suspect as potential threats to the organic
continuum of human life. They did so on religious grounds.
Projecting undesired effects on man, the East suppressed
their causes from coming into being.

The West, to the contrary, invested the continuity of human experience *in* its technologies. Aristotle warned of this danger and insisted that technics ought to be governed by ethics. But even he conceived of man's technics as something "out there."

Because of this investment of continuity in technological innovation, Western man has been historically unable to predict the effects of technology. His technologies have been the most disrupting influence in his experience of continuity. Western man has to start all over again every time a new technology replaces an older one, because of this insistence that continuity resides in technologies.

The East has been able to foresee the consequences of technologies because the East has not been very technological. Eastern religion has been hostile to technology.

A growing exception is Japan where television seems to be creating a Japanese Neuronic Man, quite as frightening as our North American variation, marked by secret mass murders and burials, and such flabbergasting murder-cum-suicide episodes as the shooting orgy in Isreal's Lod airport. Japan is the first Eastern country to experience the electronic revolution. When, amid the widespread atheism of a Japanese youth raised on television, older cultural patterns and religious beliefs return as symbol, the result may well be convulsive. We would like to think of the Lod episode, like the Manson murders, as an aberration, unlikely to reoccur. But we fear it as overture, where the murder of innocents becomes a sacrifice to some dark demon of the psyche.

The West's very technological creativity has prevented the West from foreseeing the effects of its own inventiveness. Creation is always blind. The creative act would not be irreducible novelty could its consequences be predicted in advance. Henry Ford was utterly bewildered when his Tin Lizzie tore up the agrarian world he loved. Edison preached a return to the homely virtues of Benjamin Franklin even as he helped bewitch into existence the go-go generation of today.

This blinding novelty and lack of continuity mark every technological breakthrough, but the phenomenon is accentuated by electronic technology. This accentuation, as we have suggested, is due to the abolition of the future as a projectible dimension of human experience. As indicated, every future is a past before we can even grasp it as a present on the electronic merry-go-round.

The electronic revolution truly has produced the new identification in the neuron. This neuronic identification may indeed be the principle around and within which the post-mechanical age will continue to structure itself. But this future is nothing more than an open possibility.

15 The End of Democratic Tolerance

Fair play, i.e.,taking defeat gracefully, is one with democratic citizenship. It demands a certain degree of impersonality and an acceptance of standards beyond the convictions espoused by the defeated. These standards, in traditional American politics, have been the structures and institutions built into the Constitution. Even the Civil War was a war about who interpreted correctly the written document, the Union or the Confederacy.

But no tribe --annealed into a dynastic loyalty and formed out of the flesh and bones of an internal charismatic love-- can accept as an ultimate anything beyond itself. The Blacks in America cannot do so. Those few who place country above race are sneered at for being Uncle Toms. What little is left of the white Old South anguishes between its tribal and dynastic loyalties and its belief in the law. Its older loyalties to a law and order are today interpreted not by itself but by its enemies through courts in the North.

The tribes want action right now. They want answers. Tribalization itself demands answers as instant as those demanded of a Highland laird forced to adjudicate differences between two of his clansmen quarreling about fences. The rituals of electronic participation have created the rituals of the new tribes of the "now generation" tribe of children for example, of the abolition of process and hence of democratic process in the name of a simultaneity that is literally not "natural" but electronic.

Some of these neuronic tribes today make a fetish out of not watching television. They think that TV is quite middle-class. This last is possibly television's most startling victory in its young history. To have created offspring, such as the Luddite back-to-the-land communes and the Jesus Freaks that reject electronic technology, is to ape Baudelaire's contention that the Devil's finest hour came when he convinced the nineteenth century that he did not exist.

Ideology, be it of the Left or of the Right, adjudicates every situation according to the norm of some previously understood model. The decline of ideology in our time could have been filled by religion. This did not happen. Electronic media in the Western world at large are totally defecated of serious ideology, as well as of ideology's historical enemy, religion.

The Christian insistence that man will never find absolute happiness in this world, buttressed phenomenologically by the unpleasant empirical fact that he never does, historically has prevented Christians from seeking perfect felicity here below. The Christian symbol of a "vale of tears" has been all too poignantly verified by human existence. Nonetheless, the Christian promise of eternal happiness corresponds to something equally verifiable in human existence: men simply *do* want to be happy.

185

The denial of pie in the sky necessitates a promise of pie here. This gnostic "immanentization of the eschaton"* produced ideology: i.e., the conviction that some political program could make man happy tomorrow --not today, or course. This caricature of the Christian heaven on earth has taken various forms: i.e., the Nazi Third Reich; the Russian Third Constantinople; the Marxist Classless Society; the Humanist Promise of Plenty through much Reading; the Social Engineers; Programmed Man, etc. Mr. Skinner** represents the backward glance of this reactionary messianism.

Electronic technology due to its abolition of the future as a significant dimension of human existence has destroyed secular gnosticism. Nobody can project anymore because things change so rapidly. In the Age Electric.every problem must be solved right now. It cannot be resolved in terms of some future plan which is, after all, nothing but a secular version of the Christian promise of eternal salvation. Bumper stickers stating "Don't Immanentize the Eschaton! " are a last laugh at ideology and possibly an indictment by young college students who begin to take an excessive glee in "original sin." Politics increasingly is determined by a series of priorities which cannot be reduced to ideological dreams but which can only be rendered explicable in terms of the human predicament at the moment.

16 Not a Choice but a Blur

In the United States the man with strong convictions is not always welcome. Ideological oppositions are in bad taste. Media here reflects a pre-existent situation masking differences in priorities. The decay of ideologies is taking politics out of the realm of the abstract, despite the book-oriented liberalism of its practitioners. Telepolitics is

* Eric Voeglin: *New Science of Politics.* (Chicago: University of Chicago Press, 1948)

** B.F. Skinner: *Beyond Freedom and Dignity* (New York; A. Knopf, 1971)

visceral. Viscera create an order of priority, eschewing dialectical opposition and demanding implementation.

The media masters of Mr. Nixon's 1968 telepolitical campaign presented a deliberately blurred image of their candidate, blurred to the extent that the viewer was forced to sculpture him into the candidate of his choice. It was as though the very vagueness of the candidate resembled unformed clay awaiting the hands, minds and hearts of the viewer, the sculptor. Many Nixon supporters voted for him on the strength of a television appearance on which to them he came through as a hawk --connected to *winning* the war in Vietnam. Many viewers of the same program cast their vote with the firm belief that Mr. Nixon had echoed their doveish sentiments: let's get out as quickly as we can. Mr. Nixon said as little as possible about either position, but whatever he said was applicable to both. The secret here was implementation by the viewer.

In Canada a parallel situation occurred in the spectacular political victory of the extremely telepolitical Pierre Elliott Trudeau. By refusing to promise anything, by avoiding all specifics for action in his election platform, by simply talking about generalities like "the just society" and "participatory democracy," Trudeau gathered all shades of voters to him as they projected their own specifics into the void and found Trudeau their ideal. Like Feuerbach's God, Trudeau was created in the image of those who voted for him.

In contrast, his opponent Robert Stanfield, who heads Canada's Progressive Conservative Party, is so bad on television that a fellow-politician* has remarked unkindly: "He loses 10,000 votes every time he makes a TV appearance." Standfield, a very gentle gentleman, is, in the flesh, everybody's ideal of the old-fashioned family doctor: dependable, under-

*Réal Caouette, leader of Canada's Social Credit Party, quoted in *The Gazette,* Montreal, March 17, 1972.

standing, patient and wise. But on television, he is so bland he is like a faded-out picture.

For Trudeau, however, the word "charisma" seemed invented. Certainly, the first time most Canadians ever heard the word was when it was applied to Trudeau's personal style. What will happen next time round? Since his election, he seems to have alienated many by failing to be sufficiently vague, by being too blunt ("insensitive" is the word his opponents use) about unemployment and the rising cost of living, and by turning on those who annoy him with a vulgarity and open rudeness without precedent in Canadian political life. More recently, however, some critics viewed the Nixon-Trudeau agreement on de-polluting the Great Lakes as an attempt to get back the former general support (after all, practically *everybody* is against pollution) in what may be an election year for Mr. Trudeau as well as Mr. Nixon..

Nixon and Trudeau both have telepolitical wizardry, but there is a difference. Nixon's was learned the hard way, through a series of failures and rejections; Trudeau's was natural. Nixon wanted to be President very much; Trudeau said he didn't want to be Prime Minister all that much, and he seemed so much his own man, that he was believed. Perhaps that is why, since their respective elections, Nixon has conscientiously tried to continue to be all things to all men, to keep the image sufficiently blurred to avoid antagonisms, while Trudeau often seems to be antagonizing out of private boredom or impatience. Some Canadians have voiced the suspicion that when the game of politics ceases to be fun for Trudeau, he will simply retire back to private life and take a professorship somewhere. It may be that Trudeau will give up Canada before it gives him up, for certainly, at this writing, none of his political opponents can project so strong an image.

This image imperiously demands acceptance or rejection by the electronic audience. Trudeau will have it all his own way politically or he will have it not at all. This aristocratic arrogance is splendid telepolitical theater. *He* makes the choice, not the electorate.

17 The Old Order and the Periphery

The case can be argued that local politics still follows the older chain of command. Small knots of professionals extending patronage and thus ensuring the continuation of their influence through pressure groups, are keenly bent upon either presenting or altering the status quo, as the case may be.

Local personages known at first hand are loved or hated, thanks to reputations gained and lost within the confines of the community. Political issues immediately touching upon the man paying taxes to city and county, possibly even to state, form a network of friendships built around the old Roman principle, *"Do ut des!-- I give as you give."*

This makes the political order analogous to old-fashioned horse trading.

But changes are afoot. The radical Left take-over of the Berkeley City Council is an interesting experience indicating that the revolution might succeed from the grass roots. The impact of CATV may further this trend. In any event, the movement is too young to have altered the situation significantly.

Paradoxically, mass electronic media have at least temporarily produced two antithetical effects in this area. The new media have grown up with the new rootless and nomadic population of high social mobility. This elite often lacks local ties. It occupies but never truly lives in a neighborhood. This new circulating population, certainly typical of the United States today --on top in management and education, and on bottom by the erosion of rural poor from soil to city-- is nationally and internationally oriented. It listens to Huntly-Brinkley, but not to the local news. It is fair to say that tens of millions of Americans are uninterested in what happens at home.

The prime interest of the aristocracy in the past was local. This is no longer true of the new elite. Ironically, this leaves local affairs in the hands of the partisans of the older system even while it renders that older system increasingly obsolescent.

The "temporary majority" that the mass media can create is crippled not only because this majority is carved out of a shrinking "absolute majority" in the nation; the ephemeral nature of this majority increasingly renders it impossible for the glamorized victor to govern. Based upon the image-created wizardry of television, his victory lacks the grass roots organization without which effective government over a long period of time is impossible.

Black and glamorous Senator Brooke can gain a plurailty in Irish South Boston because he looks slick and effective on TV. This does not prohibit the same electorate from voting for the racist Mrs. Hicks for mayor; nor does her following dissolve upon her failure to win the office. Based upon a careful organization that counts votes by the block, Mrs. Hicks remains a political force whether she is in or out of office.

Old-fashioned politics tends to undo the effects of Telepolitics. Wes Wise, a former television personality, wins in Dallas, thanks to his electronic image and then finds himself powerless to affect policy in the city. This is equally true of Moon Landrieu, the glamor mayor of New Orleans.

In contrast, Sam Yorty of California, who cannot quite make it in the big leagues, keeps his tight organization in splendid working order in Los Angeles and, as mayor, is able to appoint the toughest cop in the country as chief of police. Ronald Reagan, actor, is great telepolitically, but only mediocre politically.

190

Mayor Daley, pot belly and cigar, an absurd joke and caricature on television, keeps his machine running in Chicago
and governs that city tightly through a kind of participatory
democracy in which he helps his own and they help him.

The conclusion to be drawn is evident: telepolitical victories,
within the context of the shrinking majority of Americans
who are first and foremost citizens and only secondarily
tribesmen, tend to be nullified by old-fashioned politics.
Conversely, the grass roots politician with his old-fashioned
political tactics finds it impossible to be elected to significant
national offices.

The polarization has nothing essentially to do with liberal
or conservative oppositions, liberals possessing the media
and conservatives the grass roots. Reagan, after all, is both
America's most conservative political figure in big league
politics and he is also one of America's best telepoliticians.

The polarization is between non-electronic and electronic
political forms of existence. Government by the media is
still only rudimentary in the United States of America, but
government outside the media is more and more restricted
to local politics.

In the past, local news was known first. It was here.
Simultaneous national news was known later; it had to be
brought from *there* to *here*. It always arrived as history.
International news, if ever, came last.

The most famous example of this is the Battle of New Orleans,
fought valiantly after peace had been signed, or --more
recently-- a handful of Japanese soldiers in splendid isolation
fighting World War II far into the fifties, not knowing it was
over. The revolution in simultaneity has reversed all of this.
Today local political decisions and events are known later
than information bearing upon the national and international
scene. We know about the latest crisis in the French franc
before we are aware of what might be the latest crisis in

city hall. And we want to know about the French franc
before we hear about news closer to home.

A rootless and nomadic elite must live everywhere and therefore nowhere. Accustomed to following national and international news which are flashed effortlessly, this managerial
class has neither the time nor the patience to enter into
the existential density and historic idiosyncracy that per-
force constitute the symbiosis of any local poiitical situation.
It takes a lifetime of learning and living to understand what
is happening in one's own backyard, ward, or precinct. It
takes only a superficial education or no education at all
ministered by the masters of information to know through
the image what is happening everywhere in the world.

The whole world anguished over the fate of kidnapped
political figures in Quebec, but for many global television
watchers it was the first inkling that anybody outside Canada,
except seasoned Quebec watchers, or De Gaulle watchers,
had of any serious separatist problems there at all. The
decrees of Vatican II were publicized on television before
they had been promulgated by the bishops "back home":
they had not even had time to pack and get out of Rome!
(It had taken the Council of Trent some forty-six years to
make known its pronouncements.)

The older priority continues to exist only to the degree to
which politics escapes being absorbed within the newer
media. Thus, the newer media peripherally buttress the
older order by isolating it from the mainstream. This situation,
however, is temporary and most probably will not survive
the ever-increasing efficiency of mass electronic technology.

18 Captain Ludd and Harry Truman

In a sense *everybody* in a technological society is a Luddite
in that everyone likes to beat the odds and the odds are
always on the new technology. The first national campaign
to be televised, if but crudely, was the Truman-Dewey fight

of 1948. The campaign coincided with a computer-predicted landslide for Mr. Dewey. Dewey kept largely to big crowds in big cities, to filmed addresses, and to heavy print coverage. Truman made his famous whistle stop campaign through the hinterland on the traditional train with the traditional short speeches given in town after town through the midwestern hinterland in the reputed spine of the Republican Party. The *Chicago Tribune,* acting on the computer's advice and ignoring the actual early count, predicted a Dewey victory. Truman, the winner, grinningly flashed the headline over television the next morning. Man had beaten the Machine. Old-fashioned politics had won over the new. This had all the thrill of the old pro coming back and whipping the young challenger against heavy odds. Something deep in the soul of a machine-torn and gorged sensibility rejoiced.

We will not be considered spoil-sports, we trust, if we suggest that this will never happen again.

The irony of the Truman-Dewey campaign is compounded in that critics attributed Dewey's defeat to his having exuded over-confidence, to his suave and almost bland approach to politics, to his annoying consistency in what he said and how he said it. Harry Truman, the cocky bantam, with his "give 'em hell! " rhetoric, his change of moods and rhetorical styles, enormously appealed to the American electorate. Dewey was too "cool" for the late forties. Truman was "hot" enough to win, given that the U.S. political world was still "hot."

Yet it is probable that the matinee idol image plus the aura of managerial slickness of the late Thomas Dewey would have made him an admirable presidential candidate of the telepolitical world of the seventies. He was born too soon. While Truman's folksy, coaxing, country style would have rendered him the telepolitical disaster that produced the political ruin of President Lyndon Johnson, a man whose style is highly reminiscent of Harry Truman's

It is only the rare and fortunate man whose personal style coincides with the advent of a new technology. Most men are either ahead of or behind their time.

19 Participatory Totalitarianism versus the Politics of the Book

The new media are peculiarly dangerous to the United States because the country was founded on print: the Mayflower Compact, the Virginia Declarations, the Declaration of Independence, the Constitution. The nation was the book and no family went West without its Bible and many carried their Blackstone. Reaching back even farther into the American past, the Colonies had their royal, proprietary and charter documents, along with the contracts for the East India and Hudson's Bay Companies. The environment was the book. Anti-environment was nature to be conquered.

Cuba is the only country today governed by television. Castro's harangues often last four hours or more and major policy decisions are known to the TV audience before they are written down in legal documents. Castro can get away with it because Cuba is basically an oral society. They know when he is spoofing them with some grandiose four-year plan and *he* knows that *they* know. Both are in on the secret of a spoken universe they share. Cuban-Spanish is slyly conspiratorial. Participation is almost total.

What is the difference then between Telepolitics in Spain and in its offspring, Cuba?   The Communist revolution in Cuba took television seriously; the National Revolution in Spain did not.

Castro's endless addresses would be intolerable in the United States because basically a written society cannot stand all that much talk at one stretch of time. The average Nixon report on television lasts a half hour. United States sense ratios cannot take much more. But these ratios are changing rapidly. A telepolitical future may not be compatible with a political society rooted in the written word.

20 The New Luddites

If by a Luddite we mean a man who reacts against the going technology, then we must mean by a Luddite a man who is in favor of an older technology. It is absolutely impossible for anybody to be against every technology, given that man as *homo fabor* --artist-- is simply man himself. The dreadful silence in the animal's eye, Rilke's eloquent insight, is a proof that the animal cannot create, make, re-do the world. An older technology usually reaches its perfection after it has been made obsolete by a new technology.

The mounted French chivalry at Crécy and Agincourt fourteenth century, with its ironclad armor was a more perfected instrument of war than was the chain-mail clad chivalry of the previous three centuries. But whereas mail-clad knights won their battles, ironclad knights lost theirs because they faced the perfected and new technology of the English longbow and later of gunpowder.

The perfection of the large galleon came to disaster when the Spanish Armada floundered before smaller English vessels that were capable of doing more with less.

The sailing ship reached its flowering in the American clipper decades after the first crude steamship had presaged the doom of sail.

The Luddite always extols the perfection of an obsolescent technology and opposes it to the new order. The going technology is always the ground of a culture omnipresent because almost unnoticed. The obsolescent but not yet extinct technology becomes a symbolic figure, to be defended on moral or romantic grounds.

The smiling horseman triumphantly gallops past the chugging Tin Lizzie. The master of a three-masted barque in the English channel around 1890 throws a symbolic hawser to the tramp steamer tugging in his wake. Mounted Russian hussars in World War II saber to death an armored German panzer corps bogged down in the snows of the Ukraine.

The Luddite, popular belief to the contrary, is *not* anti-technological. He is passionately in favor of the older technology against the newer. William Morris, in rejecting the paleolithic industrialization of the late nineteenth century, attempted to resurrect the most delicate and perfected forms of printing books by hand. This hero of the historian of technology, Lewis Mumford, defended and resurrected an older technology against a newer.

The passionate defense of "the book" encountered everywhere in the United States, manifested most especially in the bizarre resurrections of humanistic education, i.e. Mortimer Adler and Robert Hutchins in heavily-financed "Great Books" foundations are evidences that the book is no longer a taken-for-granted ground of our society, but rather a romantically-defended symbolic figure.

Attacks against technological dehumanization are made by literary gentlemen who hop from city to city and hall to hall, thanks to computer-directed jet aircraft. Sweet treason against the going technological order is whispered over telephone by traitors in Los Angeles who speak to traitors in Washington. The Luddite defenders of older technologies have to use the newer. Where did you hear the last attack on television? Probably on educational TV.

The same can be said of S.D.S., Black Panthers, and other instruments of the radical left. They do not possess the new media. They do not like the new media, but they need the new media. Therefore, the New Leftist attitude remains ambiguous.

196

21 Far Right Drop Outs

The most magnificent drop-out generations are not found
on the Left but on the far Right. A more classical attitude
towards a new technology represented by defenders of an
older technology is to be found in the print-oriented far Right
in the United States, the ultra-conservative movements
identified with Orange County, the Constitutional Alliance,
H.L. Hunt and "Lifeline," Dan Smoot, and the John Birch
Society. The newly-establishmentalized conservatism of
the *National Review* straddles both worlds, electronic and
non-electronic. By and large these millions of Americans,
whose hero remains Barry Goldwater, and possibly Governor
Ronald Reagan, are in the mainstream of American affluence.
They are wealthy, but their wealth is not in the media. They
are capable of broad political action, but they have chosen
to act politically largely in abstraction from the new electronic
media and from the older and more respectable organs of
print media. Mr. J. Evetts Haley's book *A Texan Looks at
Lyndon* sold well into the millions, but it is fair to say
that nobody totally immersed in the going media ever heard
of the book. It was reviewed almost nowhere. The same
phenomenon occurred with Phyllis Shafley's *A Choice Not
an Echo* and John Stormer's *None Dare Call It Treason,*
ground out in cheap paperback editions by ad hoc printing
houses. The presence of these books represents a new underworld print medium, totally divorced from older established
print medium which largely (but not always) works in har-
mony with the newer electronic modes of communication.
Thus there has been created an underworld press of the Right
which parallels the underworld press of the far Left: *The
Berkeley Barb, Notes from the Underground, Rolling Stone,*
and *Evergreen.*

Both extremes of the new "out" media exhibit formally
identical characteristics. Both believe in absolutes, be they
the puritan ethic or sexual liberty. Both divide the universe
into the saved and the damned, be the saved patriots or rebels
(or be the damned the projected vision of their own sub-

conscious that each sees in his dialectical opposite). The
S.D.S. passed out nearly two million leaflets during the
1968 "Spring War." James Kunen was absolutely correct
in his short article on this "mimeograph revolution" in
Esquire. * Leaflets are a major media force on the student
today. "A smudgy mimeographed sheet is strongly
associated with powerlessness and a lack of funds which
is good, because broad segments of American society can
identify with that condition. The leaflet is the recognized
organ of the 'outs.' " Then what about the leaflets of be-
sieged college officials? What has happened to the un-
precedented data that they have published for students?
Kunen goes on to point out that they come off as
proclamations instead of communications. The "form" of
administration leaflets lacks shabbiness; it is too neat.

Leaflets from both extremes of far Right and far Left seem
to have declined in the early seventies as neuronic identity
became more and more interiorized. The leaflet war suggested
an effort to convert and to combat. Conversion and combat-
iveness are giving way to the strategy of survival, Neuronic
Man's substitute for messianism.

22 America: Wounded, Hurt and Isolationist

The Vietnam experience, its failures and frustrations,
would be enough to cause the most bellicose of nations
to pause and consider its ways. For the United States
--a country that has liked to play the moral hero in lead
roles on the world stage-- to lose out, both morally and
militarily, to bit players is particularly ignominious. Like
all who are disgraced publicly, we want to retire and
reconsider what next.

The expulsion of Nationalist China from the United Nations
provided a theatrical demonstration of our loss of face, as

*Kunen, James Simon, "The Mimeograph Revolution," *(Esquire,*
September 1969) p.102

198

delegates from the Third World gleefully leaped to their feet and broke into tumultuous applause at our embarrassment. It all hastens the new implosive isolationism.

Isolationism since World War II has not been a respectable stance among American liberals. Their problem was how to get the U.S. to interfere only, and always, on the side of "good" and "democracy." It was a tricky challenge, since not only do various peoples in various nations have varied ideas on what's good for them, but even in the United States, Americans have been far from unanimous over whether capitalist dictators or Communist dictatorships are the more "democratic." In the dilemma, the official U.S. government attitude has been the pragmatic one: support our "friends."

Although American liberals now seem as isolationist as everybody else, they still feel uneasy with it --as well they should, since nineteenth century isolationism is no longer possible. Hence Senator George McGovern, in calling America home, still wishes to present a good-natured face to the world and assure it of our goodwill, implying that goodwill can still solve problems. But telepolitical decentralization has ended such simplistic solutions for our time.

Naziism may have provided America with its last opportunity to have an enemy we could, wholeheartedly and almost unanimously, hate.

Mr. Nixon confessed himself shocked at the tribal U.N. behavior over the expulsion of Nationalist China. So too was the stiff, proud and aristocratic clan of the U.S. Senate. But today, friendships shift overnight. Dr. Henry Kissinger, in an irony almost too good for art and found only in history, returned from Peking the morning after the People's Republic of China was admitted to the U.N. and Taiwan was expelled. The subject of his conversation that morning with the President was the President's then-proposed trip to Peking.

199

23 Governing the Chaos

With the United States withdrawing into financial as well as political isolation, the explosive drive toward internationalism has been diffused. The new gray eminences govern implosively in order that the weakened national state might simply *survive.*

The question of discontinuous grouping ultimately has little to do with victory and nothing to do with the victory of ideology. The Germanic tribes that settled into the centralized Roman Empire were fleeing fiercer tribes from Asia. The Indians on the great American plains turned on the white man because he had stolen tribal lands, thus threatening their very way of life. The Scottish clansmen that rallied to the Stuarts in the Jacobite wars tended to melt back into their Highland strongholds.

The tribe succeeds politically when it maintains itself in existence as a viable social order.

The march of a conquering ideology such as Marxism or the victorious Revolution in France inevitably de-tribalized and centralized its adherents within monolithic blocks of men who acted on the command of soviets or triumvirates or the single leader. But the essentially conservative nature of clans and tribes is introverted and even solipsistic. To have won the palm of victory, it suffices that the group continue to exist: that the blood line be handed down; that the cherished way of life be.

This new neuronic conservatism, actually a panic before po sible annihilation, manifests itself everywhere. The ecology crisis is a cosmic reflection of the unrest that stirs beneath the surface of conscious rationality in our day. The denial that science can tinker any longer with our dwindling resources without being subjected to political control is today as much a first principle of discourse as was science's right

to expand indefinitely a first principle of the progressivism
of the past.

The national state, battered by new "nations" and separat-
isms shares with them all *one* ultimate passion: the national
state would survive as well, if it could!

The state no longer believes in the older ideologies whose
vehicle for missionary expansion the state once was.

24 The End of Internationalism

Internationalism as an ideal has suffered the fate of all the
older messianic politics. Internationalism is a fuzzy and
archaic hangover, a late-late show reminiscent of the ideals
of the mid-forties.

The internationalist presumed that the abolition of nationalism would do away with hatred and injustice between men,
but the new tribalism has created new hatreds and new forms
of injustice. The new technology forces a global interdepen-
dence confronting man with man; this removes neither
hatred nor injustice; on the contrary, it makes them all the
more glaring.

Radio brought back cannibalism in the Congo. Cambodian
troops decorate their tents with the heads of their enemies.
So too did a few United States Marines in World War II in
the Pacific --but nobody saw them do it!   Today the heat
of the global light is on everybody that a camera can reach.
The new technology confronts every man with every other
man.

This has little to do with the spatial crowding of population
explosion. The population implosion is such that were there
only a million people on the face of the earth they would
react to one another as do the inhabitants of Faulkner's
quasi-mythical Yoknapatawpha County.

The human and technical problems involved in governing this chaotic situation are such that no head of a democratic state can afford to depend on institutions fashioned in and for the nineteenth century. He must, in the very discharge of whatever oath an antiquated Constitution might lay on him, turn to the super-group, the think-tank, the gray eminence.

He must link this with the skillful PR tactics of the gnomes of the image as they fashion fluid group alliances as well as divide in order to conquer.

The new Goths and Huns are not at the gates. There are no more gates in a world in which everything is center and nothing is periphery. It takes more than genius to govern such a universe, one of total discontinuity.

The national state is doomed by history, but its death can be postponed as can a terminal cancer by the intelligent exercise of technical expertise. The clinical cold-bloodedness of technocracy weds the glamor of the telepolitical show. The statesman has left to him only one task: that of acting as marriage counselor to both.

Part IV
Secret Governments

To govern today in America means to do two opposing
things: (1) to gain power and to sustain oneself in power
through the use of Telepolitics: (2) to exercise that power
behind the electronic glare. This requires government
through, and increasingly by, "specialists" who have not
been elected but on whom those elected depend.

1 The One-Way Window

A theory much advocated by management consultants in the
fifties insisted that employees could be kept happy simply if
their grievances were listened to. Improvement was not
necessary. You didn't actually have to do anything about
them, just listen to them and give the impression that you
cared. Politicians in both the United States and Canada have
been doing this for the last thirty years. They answer mail.
But constituents are well-advised not to follow up with a
second letter and expect an answer. It is almost bad taste
to pursue an issue once you have been told that you have
been heard.

Television projects the illusion that all grievances are being
heard, listened to, even as it informs the nation of grievances
the nation did not know it had.

A group or an individual with grievances ignored by the media has a true grievance indeed!

In the mechanical age, centralized political power receives information needed to rule through bureaucratic arteries which terminated in the remote blood capsules of township, county and parish. Information flowed uphill, only to be purified and distilled of everything superfluous as it approached the centers of power.

In turn, both commands and laws were established from on top and promulgated below through a staggered series of communication networks which depended essentially on the written word. The chain of command meshed with a chain of petition in which public sentiment made itself known initially to local politicians, finally to the capital. A dialogue was thus established between ruler and ruled.

Today an anomalous situation exists in which power is omnipresent but in which the very authority supposedly incarnated in a democratic society remains atomized. No centralized government structure in the old-fashioned way can possibly attend to, let alone satisfy, the conflicting desires of tribes which are so foreign to one another that they are marked less by mutual hostility than by mutual incomprehension.

Television as a totalitarian instrument as in Cuba, or as an ill-begotten ugly sister as in Europe, can endure only if television can be prevented from emerging from its primitive state. Such an emergence promises neither democracy nor totalitarianism but rather --as we have argued throughout these pages-- an implosive unraveling and re-weaving of the social fabric of any culture.

This current feedback blockage at the present primitive state of the "sleeping giant" of television will certainly suffer substantial change with the advent of CATV, cable TV and satellite television, due before the end of the decade. Thus far, however, the telepolitical age has caused a breakdown

of the classical chain of command process from top to
bottom, from governor to governed, with no comparable
breakthrough from governed to governor.

2 Representative Government as Conversation

Where there is a conversation between government and
people, representative rule is a possibility. Historically, no
government that existed in a void has endured for very long.
The void has been filled by revolution as in Russia, 1917, or
by the emergence of a new *de facto* government which
ruled in the name of the empty husks of a *de jure*
legitimacy.

The Merovingian kings, heads addled with insanity or
stupidity, were trundled through the streets in carts;
Turkish sultans were caged in harems filled by concubines
who destroyed in their supposed masters all insight into
any outside reality. They were pleasured into oblivion.

Representation demands that the prince make his decisions
after he has heard every side of the case. Thus Sir John
Fortescue insisted that the King of England was never higher in his power than when he was *in* Parliament.

The new telepolitical situation permits *them* to talk to us
without seeing us, whereas we *see* them but cannot talk to
them. The increasing violence and barbarization of American
and Canadian society makes it a risk for a prince ever to be
in his realm. He might be, and has been, shot!

The increasing isolation of the American President in the
White House has made it necessary for him to gather round
his person a group of technicians, experts who represent no
one in any judicial sense of the term but who bring to the
heart of power the brains without which power cannot
function.

205

These "brains" often make colossal goofs as in the case of
CIA intelligence given Kennedy before the Bay of Pigs and
the more recent Rand think-tank advice on the Vietnam war
as disclosed in the Pentagon Papers.

The danger of the think tank is precisely its lack of account-
ability to any representative institution.

Nonetheless, a chief of state cannot govern without the advice
of the new technocrats. Without the technocrats the chief
of state or of government is nothing other than a prefabricated telepolitical fantasy. Only thus can he escape the
burden of being nothing more than the image into which the
imagemakers have fashioned him.

3 Ads versus Issues

Senator George McGovern is a good ad man. He aims at
administering a regrouping of Americans. The only trouble
is that to administer is not the same as to govern. At best
he compliments Wallace --a kind of Wallace of the Left--
because both have their feet on the same ground.

McGovern can only touch those who have no place to go;
Wallace, those who want to go no place. Both are no
more than backward waves of the future. They are figures
loving in the ruins, one another and their past dreams. The
unsuspecting climax is that figures topple as grounds shift.

Bringing America home and putting everyone back to work
is a nostalgic remembrance of times past. But our work
will not work for us anymore. Any attempt to structure
the diverse and discontinuous neuronic dreams and inten-
tions through a process of integration into united action
is obsolete. Radical homogenization in any party
platform is doomed to failure because there is no broad
national base for homogenization in the telepolitical ground.

206

Voters are no longer able to subsist on the partially-digested nutrition of party platforms. They want personalities, not issues. This was poignantly demonstrated by "Eagleton's week" in late July of 1972. As the news media and party-pushers proceeded to eat young Senator Eagleton alive, no one commented that it had been by far the most attention the Democrats had received in years, outside their conventions. The pleading from such columnists as James Reston was for dumping Eagleton and thus escaping from "personalities" and returning back to "issues."

But no such return is possible. Just as ads are not meant for conscious consumption, the iconic image of the telepolitician has almost nothing to do with issues.

Organizations such as the Washington-based Accuracy in Media group, a non-partisan organization whose aims are --among many-- the improvement of accuracy in news reporting, are the best possible allies for government by personality and super-groups. They wave Article IV, Section 23 of the Television Code of the National Association of Broadcasters at CBS after "The Selling of the Pentagon." It states: "No program shall be presented in a manner which through artifice or simulation would mislead the audience as to any material fact."

By this rigid criterion no telepolitical candidate could be allowed to appear in a televised campaign for office. As long as content or "accuracy" hypnosis can be induced as a diversionary tactic, the iconic ad form of the telepolitician can do its most effective work and the iconic functions most effectively when it is not noticed consciously and when the rabbit of issues keeps the critical intelligence from noticing what is really going on: i.e., an act of governing *through* telepolitical magic *by* men who hover, hidden behind the tube.

4 Telepolitics: Government by Personality

Telepolitics --government by personality-- can never be more effective than when these personalities put over the myth that something else is at stake, namely, accuracy in media. This diversionary tactic is a highly effective smoke-screen permitting the telepolitical personality to consult with his super-groups, absorb their advice, decide, and govern by fiat. The issue has nothing to do with "accuracy." The issue is *power*.

In the new personalized and stylized world of Telepolitics, issues have become as irrelevant as are curricula in the university. What the student remembers is *who* said it and *how* did he say it, not *what* he said.

The shabbiest of curricula can be rendered brilliant if passed through the prism of splendid teachers. The most excellent of curricula fail if taught by mediocre professors. A year later, the student remembers --if he remembers anything at all-- the teacher and not the content of the course.

Analogously, the telepolitical personality wins or loses --telepolitically. The content of his program is largely beside the point.

The late Senator Dirksen of Illinois bitterly complained that his indispensable efforts as minority whip towards passing the Civil Rights Bill would not gain him a single Negro vote; but neither did it lose him any votes in his Re-publican and conservative constituency that was less than enthusiastic about the legislation which Dirksen made his very own during the Johnson administration.

It is unimportant whether a man thinks or votes liberal or conservative or radical. What matters is a conservative or liberal or radical *image*. The image is the carrot. And the democratic masses follow the carrot. This is true of ele-phants as well as donkeys.

208

Philip Berrigan, interviewed February 2, 1972, during jury selection for his impending trial, explained to the press that while he was not guilty as accused, the trial would nevertheless get the issues before the American people. This is highly peripheral to getting Father Berrigan before the American people. The *issue* over television is the Berrigan *image*.

5 Super-Groups: Government behind the Governor

In order to govern in a representative fashion, the prince must talk to the people. When he no longer talks to the people, he must talk to someone else. The gray eminence is an old historical phenomenon. When Louis XIII could no longer talk to France because his ancestors had crushed all the autonomous institutions through which Frenchmen had been accustomed to dialogue with their kings, Louis XIII talked to Richelieu. That Richelieu soon began to do most of the talking seems to have been the trick that history plays on princes who fear their people.

Even the men behind the throne often need their own shadow conscience or technical expertise. A striking instance is given us in the German General Staff in World War I. General von Hindenburg was the national hero, the victor of Tannenberg; his face --the face of every German father-- later swept him to the presidency of the Weimar Republic despite his royalist grumblings. But General Ludendorff was the brains behind von Hindenburg and behind Ludendorff stood the grayest of all eminences, Hoffmann, the brains of the brains of the public image.

History reveals very few Oliver Cromwells who talk things out directly with God.

Politics, as we have known the art in modern times, is ambivalent in that it englobes two often-antithetical talents, the capacity to gain and to retain power plus the capacity to govern. The man with the charisma needed to get and hold power does not necessarily have any talent for government at all.

Expertise brilliance in the art of government is impatient with procedures, uneasy in society, and generally inept at the fashion show which accompanies political life.

In the Middle Ages, power --in theory, at least-- belonged to the king, but he could exercise that power only by consulting the authority that reposed in a highly structured and autonomous society.

In the age of absolutism, both power and authority were centered in the crown, but the kings found it necessary to rely on cabinets composed of technically competent secretaries who often vied with one another for the royal favor.

In the age of classical parliamentary democracy, the chief of government was simultaneously a party leader and he could rise above party loyalty and advise only at great risk to his chances for re-election.

Although the man behind the scenes, admitted into the closet of the king through the back door, is a common *dramatis persona* of history, today the mind in the closet really has come into its own.

The men who make up the super-government must *initially* stay off television. Yet this transference of power from representative institutions to unseen experts has not escaped the antennas of dedicated revolutionaries such as the Berrigan brothers. Their reported plans did not concern a supposed plot to kidnap Vice President Agnew, the Speaker of the House, or even the commanding general of the armed forces. Why Henry Kissinger? What electorate did Kissinger represent, anyway?

Henry Kissinger could travel to Peking and Paris in secret because he is, or was until recently, anonymous.

The success of any super-group lies in the anonymity of the men who make it up. This anonymity does not exist in political circles. No one close to the ruling head of state is anonymous to the dedicated politician whose profession demands that he be a busybody. The anonymity is tele-political, on the new electronic stage, and on that stage the members of the super-group appear only as a blurred muted chorus as in early Greek drama, identifiable by their presence, yet unidentifiable by this very presence. They wear the mask, the *persona,* of the dynastic leader.

Men of this nature fill the vacuum when government is re-moved from the governed and when the throne finds itself isolated. A striking instance of this today is the super-group known as the *Opus Dei* which dominates Franco's govern-ment. Lyndon Johnson had his Walter Jenkins, Richard Nixon has Henry Kissinger. Trudeau has a super-group headed by his Secretary, former Montreal lawyer Marc Lalonde, that is said to be so powerful that if you want something from Government in Canada, they --and not the members of Parliament or even the members of the Cabinet-- are the ones to see.

The obsolescence of representative democracy was dramati-cally evidenced when Mr. Nixon met Chairman Mao accom-panied by Henry Kissinger. Presumably the Secretary of State, Mr. Rogers, was cooling his heels somewhere else in Peking. The members of the American press in China supposedly knew where he was. Wherever he was, however, he was not televised. Mr. Rogers was the great non-event of the Peking caper, referred to by *Newsweek* as the first McLuhanesque summit.

Two months later when Mr. Nixon paid an official visit to Canada, a still further dimension was suggested. Just before the visit *The Montreal Star* ran a story saying that when

211

Mr. Nixon would be meeting Mr. Trudeau for talks in Ottawa, the only other persons who would be present were Mr. Kissinger and a Canadian by the name of Ivan Head, a man virtually unknown to the Canadian public but whose advice Mr. Trudeau had been getting on foreign affairs. Whether this meeting that cut out both the U.S. Secretary of State, Mr. Rogers and the Canadian Secretary of External Affairs, Mitchell Sharp, actually took place, the paper did not tell us. But the mere suggestion that it *could* take place is enough to disturb all who still believe that those elected ought to be the ones who make policy.

The bursting of Kissinger into the public glare even to his varied and glamorous night life around Washington is a dramatic instance of the new telepolitical dynasticism. The counsellors and friends of the prince are his own trusted vassals and their influence weighs more in the affairs of state than do men who represent institutions rather than men.

The gradual divorce of those who have the ear of the ruling dynast from pre-existent representative structures is pro- ducing two antithetical effects: (l) the secret counsellor becomes public and thus joins the telepolitical show; (2) willy-nilly, he must perform under the electronic glare and therefore his older role will be assumed by another --unknown and unseen.

The success of technical expertise is crowned with the palm of public acclaim and hence ceases to be itself.

Objectivity demands anonymity but anonymity yearns to transcend itself. This infinite regress is consubstantial with a world in which the puppeteer would be puppet.

The influence of these men wax and wane because they form a loose group composed of technocrats surrounding the public repository of power and each technocrat looks first to his own career. In order to govern a televised empire where televised access of the nation to the state does not exist, the telepolitical statesman must necessarily create this governing arm that transcends older mechanical structures hampering his freedom of action. The governing clique must be extra-institutional and thus free to act for the sake of the leader's image and continued success. It is responsible only to the leader, not to the electorate.

6 Richard Nixon: Telemagician

Who is H.R. Haldeman? Few outside Washington political circles know the name. For three years the nation neither heard nor saw him.

On February 7,8 and 9, 1972, NBC's *Today* show announced a first, three interviews with Mr. H.R. Haldeman, assistant to President Nixon. The filmed interviews, conducted by Barbara Walters, monstrated Mr. Haldeman to the watching nation. He is a man who has been called a very private person as well as one of the most powerful men in the White House. It is he who decides who sees (and who does *not* see) the President, and he is in charge of all the papers that go to (and do *not* go to) the President's desk. (M. Lalonde has the same privileged position in Canada.) It was Mr. Haldeman's first television appearance.

Having Henry Kissinger on the cover of *Time* (February, 1972) and Haldeman on the *Today* show would seem to destroy the anonymity needed by the super-group to effectively act. Yet it is brilliant telepolitical strategy by the new telemagician, Richard Nixon.

We must bear in mind that these powerful men have been more or less "under wraps" for three years. In an election year Mr. Nixon has everything to gain and nothing to lose by letting us all have a look-see into the inner workings of his surround.

213

The fascination engendered by television for process is illustrated superbly by these examples. The governed are not so preoccupied at *what* is done by its elected representatives, as *how* they do it. The vicarious participation in who-we-are-not-but-would-like-to-be obliterates the old reasoned debate over issues. The men around Mr. Nixon are by now more interesting than Mr. Nixon himself.

If Mr. Nixon wins the 1972 presidential election his super-group are politically secure for the next four years. If he loses the election, the super-group dissolves and returns to non-political life or other political careers.

In Canada, indications are that members of Mr. Trudeau's super-group are about to emerge on the political stage, including the head of the group, Mr. Lalonde.

Running individuals one would like to have in one's Cabinet in "safe seats" is a time-honored custom of Canadian political leaders. Sometimes such men have never even seen, let alone lived in, the constituency they are suddenly "parachuted" into. While it is scarcely grass-roots democracy, the constituents not only don't seem to mind; they are usually delighted, for it means they will have a representative on Parliament Hill very close to the center of power.

In the United States, the super-group emerges at the close of Mr. Nixon's first four year term to *do* his telepolitical campaigning for him --at no expense we might add to Republican campaign coffers. What Henry Kissinger does is *news*, national and Republican news. Who Haldeman is and how he functions is even more dramatic news because we have never before heard of him.

The super-group plays its dramatic role in throwing up a "media barrier" to other presidential aspirants. A "media barrier" may mean many things, but the most elementary aspect as it substantially concerns Telepolitics is that when you are watching one show, you are not watching another.

214

Presidential hopefuls scramble for some magic moment that will catapult them onto the electronic stage. It is becoming almost impossible to upstage an incumbent president and his advisors.

When Nixon arrived in Peking February 21, 1972 the event was telecast instantly via a 1.6 million dollar communications trailer in the Chinese capital, an Intelsat TV satellite in the Pacific sky, a communications station in Amesburg, California and a transcontinental cable to New York --into millions of homes around the globe.

Three super Hercules planes flew more than fifty tons of communications equipment January 28 to Peking, most of it necessary for television. Mr. Nixon wrote in his book *Six Crises,* that "where votes are concerned, a paraphrase of what Mr. Krushchev claims in an 'ancient Russian proverb' could not be more controlling: 'One TV picture is worth 10,000 words.' "

The new Nixon is the telepolitical Nixon. A private man uncomfortable with media, he learned his lesson from John Kennedy, a man completely at home under the lights. The fact that the Republican party spent over twelve million dollars on media during the 1968 presidential campaign as compared to six spent by the Democrats is its own medium as message.

Mr. Nixon at first glance seems to be the exception to all emerging telepolitical symbolism. A Horatio Alger man from the classic myth of Americana, he nevertheless created his own dynastic myth before the eyes of the nation during his first presidential term.

Precarious in his relation to media, he has brilliantly demonstrated an awareness of his shaky position by anticipating what had to be done by any president in order for him or the nation to survive. In Telepolitics the only defense is an ongoing offense. The show must go on.

215

7 World Government versus Secret Government

Ni Jésus, Ni Marx sees only one possible outcome of the
second world revolution: world government. This prediction
must seem highly probable to any sophisticated philosopher
of culture whose orientation is dominated by print. To a man
with the humanistic background and education of author
Revel, the late twentieth century looks like an extension
and confirmation of the predictions and dreams of earlier
gnostic prophets of revolution: betrayed in Russia and China,
impossible of fulfillment in basically conservative France, the
revolution is about to explode within the United States.

In good French Cartesian fashion, Revel lists five conditions
for revolution and finds them fulfilled only in the United
States. From the United States, presumably, the revolution
will spread everywhere and a secularist world government will
be brought into existence by this conquest from the streets.
But Revel --and he is peculiarly illustrative of our point
because he is not totally insensitive to the effects of electronic
technology-- fails to see what is patently there before his eyes
to see: i.e., the homogenous mass necessary for any second
American Revolution, to say nothing of the world government which would issue therefrom, has been broken up by
the new technology and, most especially, by television.

The world moves not towards world government but
towards an anarchy whose closest historical parallel is the
epoch following the fall of Rome and preceding the
Carolingian Empire.

The conclusion that Revel, and others like him, ought to draw
is the death of the democratic national state.

World government can never be exercised upon a whirling
dust of clans. If the national state is caving in, this does not
mean it is giving way to the supra-national state.

To argue in this fashion is analogous to arguing that increasing poverty in the moderately well-off is a forerunner of affluence. The reasoning holds no water logically.

Revel fails to understand that the only revolution the United States is likely to undergo would be a counter-revolution from a newly tribalized right wing whose patience had finally broken under the weight of street violence, insecurity, and accumulated frustration.

Do we suffer, at the price of avoiding a nuclear war between super states, the daily post-atomic wars of our pock-marked cities? or the most frightening war of all --the survival of the fittest, every man for himself?

World federalists and others have looked upon the United Nations as the logical stepping stone to world government. Had the decentralizing effects of electronic technology not shattered the centralization inherent in mechanization, it is highly probable that the next decade would have seen the United Nations or some comparable body converted into a world government, a government initially benign towards continental and local differentiations, but ultimately as hostile to such idiosyncracies as is machine technology itself.

The structuring of the United Nations in San Francisco reflected this very mechanical bias --one vote for each nation-- with a veto for one of the Big Five. The impossibility of meshing the principle of national sovereignty with democratic majoritarianism has been demonstrated time and again in that body.

The giant corporation has moved beyond the time where "home offices" had "branch offices" abroad, American firms with interests in Canada, South America, Europe, etc. The very concept of a center for a business corporation today is obsolete because the entire organization can be governed from any "point" on the globe, and that "point" can be as

217

temporary as a hotel room. Howard Hughes' much
publicized wanderings around the world illustrate dramati-
cally what is becoming a commonplace. The national
state, at least in the United States, is further threatened by
the multi-national corporation because prohibitive tax
legislation is causing a flight of money across obsolete
national frontiers.

Each multi-national corporation forms its own neuronic
"space" which is constituted by a tissue of interlocking
interests only peripherally related today to what used to be
the "home office." These corporations may very well become --some may already be-- far more powerful than
national governments, self-constituting commerical tribes
with their own style of life, their own neuronic identities
and loyalties. Given that the multi-national corporation
functions within the electronic rim-spin, it wraps the old
national state within itself. It thus becomes a super-
political power, or --better yet-- a network of super-
political powers upon which national states are increasingly dependent and before which they are increasingly
powerless.

Only world government could control these commercial
and industrial giants, and world government is a dream of
the past.

8 The Think Tank as Dunce

Once upon a diatribe the numbers game was invented. It
was played for over three hundred years. Playing was forgotten several hundred years ago. The Eureka point was
discovered by a man splashing about in a pool, but Herman
Kahn is not Archimedes.

When some fat foundation grant, further engorged by Uncle's
grease, invites a handful of scholars to sit down and think by
the numbers, there is born "the Think Tank." Relieved from
all daily routines except that of "thinking," they are in the

position of Hegel's "Thought." What does "Thought" do?
Well, it *thinks.*

This well-paid thinking for the sake of thinking, an elephan-
tine exercise, brings forth a mouse in effect; e.g., Herman
Kahn's predictions about the year 2000, which almost
equaled the shrewd observations of any intelligent observer
of the evening news in 1967 concerning what would happen
in 1968.

Think-tanksmen are great on statistics. In Washington, they
fed statistical data into a computer which subsequently predicted that the human race would end in one hundred years
unless we learned to live ascetically and have fewer babies.
Little can be said about the "fewer babies" but the advice
to live ascetically was made by men gathered together in
Washington whose individual fees for two weeks' work by-
pass the national average income for a year's labor.

Statistics are the stock-in-trade of these high-living proponents of the simple life.

Are statistics a device of those who would utilize everything
in terms of the past?   Are statisticians static status seekers
accounting for everything?   Is the boom in statistics at
present a frenzied utilization of yesterday's precept which
attempts to limit electronic comprehension to computation?

Will statistics fade since those who count are losing their
status?   After all, quantification is noetic in its structuring,
while the character of the structure of the universe is
resonance: i.e., poetic.

Contemporary think tanks represent rationalism's finest
hour. Using all the techniques of electronic revolution,
think-tanksmen exercise them in old-fashioned mechanical
isolation. Therefore their predictions can as often as not
be calamitously beside the point. The Peter Principle

219

applies here: think-tanksmen have risen to such a peak of technical excellence that they are out of the action.

In their attempt to be "objective," they have lost sight of the participatory structure of the Age Electric. The Rand think-tank people in advising the Pentagon on the Vietnam War certainly abstracted that war from the nation's television sets. The media's role in the war was the x factor absent from their equations. Media was the army they did not notice.

Power must use think-tanksmenship because the organs of representative democracy can count only one thing --votes. But power were well advised to administer the proverbial grain of salt to technocratic advice.

Napoleon's having the "blahs" may well have determined the course of events at Waterloo. The murder of Mao Tse-tung's first wife may very well have determined his entire career. James II's nose bleed before Salisbury may have made the Glorious Revolution. Hitler's drugged sleep linked with his insistence that he not be disturbed *and* his insistence that three crack panzer divisions not be moved without his personal command made possible the success of the Allied landing on D-Day. What would have happened had von Stauffenberg's bomb-laden briefcase not been inadvertently kicked and then moved a foot from where he had put it down in the Wolf's Lair on July 20, 1944?

Poets have always understood this. They have long pondered the escalating dangers of the loss of "a horseshoe nail" and how awry can go "the best laid plans of mice and men." They know that "there are more things in heaven and earth" than are dreamed of in any philosophy.

The gift of statesmanship involves the capacity to seize the intangible, the non-computerizable, the density and mystery of existence, the irrational, the poetic --and use them to weld together "information" and "facts," so that

220

the totality transcends all of the data that has gone to make it up.

Government by technocracy, if pushed to its logical extremes, could be destroyed by an enemy who understood the simple trick of acting in an irrational way.

Conclusion

1 Misunderstanding Media

Understanding Media by Marshall McLuhan was an international best seller. Yet ten years after its publication no
one seems to understand media. We fumble and suffer its
effects, while the media cast their mushrooming cloud over,
around, under and *in* global man.

The basic failure to understand the new media is the consequence of an almost total ignorance of its epistemological
structure. Having grown up in the United States of America,
a profoundly pragmatic and unphilosophical nation, the
media have largely failed to find their own philosophers.
Our general approach to the new electronic media is or-
chestrated by a naive realism. Everyone still thinks of the
act of knowing --of every act of knowing-- as though it
were a matching of images and ideas with reality. This
representationalist theory goes back to John Locke and
the origins of English empiricism.

Naive realism looks upon knowing as though it were parallel
to snapping a photograph. To know is to produce a copy
of grandma for the family album. The better the resem-
blance, the better the photograph. According to Locke's
representationalism, the mind is a picture book which is perfect to the degree to which it eschews novelty and sticks to

the business of reporting visually that which once was. To know is to freeze the fluidity of the real into a static pictorial mosaic. Even writing then becomes frozen speech.

A good contrast is Aristotle's theory of knowledge. Everything in the content of knowledge is the contribution of the thing known.

In a sense when Jews and Nazis knew Adolf Hitler, it was the same Adolf Hitler they knew. There was no distinction in content. In another sense, it was not the same Adolf Hitler at all. Jews knew him in a mode of being annealed in pain, suffering, and persecution. Nazis knew him in a mode of being in which he was received as a charismatic leader and the hope of the fatherland.

Everything in knowledge as an act done, as a performance, is the contribution of the *knower*. *"Quid quid recipitur recipitur ad modum recipientis.* --Whatever is received, is received according to the mode of the recipient." Knowledge is essentially man's identity with the world and his diversity from the world through his having received that world according to his mode of existence in space and time. Knowledge, both sensual and intellectual, is the identification of knower and known.

Media of communication are not mere neutral instruments that transmit messages presumed to be previously unformed or structured by these same media. Every message is already formed initially within tissues of imagery distended into concepts and judgments.

Misunderstanding about knowledge produced a massive misunderstanding in the political order: i.e., issues somehow antidated their being communicated and these issues somehow existed before they existed in communications.

The Encyclopedists talked about the Rights of Man as though they pre-existed historical man who never finds himself outside a network of communication systems which render him at every moment of his life a social and political animal.

Representationalism suggests that reality is a linear trajectory composed of: (a) content; (b) transmission belt or medium; (c) communicated effect out in "the real world " of Newtonian space. This philosophical farsightedness simply makes it impossible to understand what media are.

Media are forms which structure every act of knowing. Every message is identical with its being communicated. There is no sound in the forest if there is no receptor. And even within the intimacy of the self, no one has anything to communicate until he has communicated it at least to himself. Understanding is one with its articulation. The Christian tradition discovered this in its insistence that "In the beginning was the Word." Earlier the Greeks had spoken of the Logos as a "gathering" or "togethering" of the real which was one with its articulation in speech and thought. A "pure meaning" or "message" outside of some communication system is a fantasy.

2 The Causal Fallacy

The *failure* to understand that the being of any message communicated is formally caused by the gestalt, or structure of the medium of communication, that it would be other than it is in any other form, belongs to the very common syndrome of predicting that things which have already happened are about to happen. The insistence that violent behavior of youth and other tribes is going to barbarize America unless we rapidly do something about it puts the cart before the horse. America is already barbarized.

It seems incredible that the older generation with its rigidly adhered-to forms of content would learn so quickly to accept their children taking drugs, growing beards, getting dirty, not working, not joining the army, resisting the draft,

225

etc. *Has television conditioned both young and old to these realities?* Is the "generation gap" then a necessary techno-logical interface between the older fading mechanical tech-nology and the new electric age?

Violent behavior grows out of violent being. The play-acting that people are getting ready either to "rebel" against the system or to react against the rebellion is a fallacy of the misplaced consequent. A conclusion is made to take the place of a premise. Sensitivity training groups pyramided in deadly seriousness into schooled existence in 1968 after the whole nation had been radically soaked in sensitivity. Women's Liberation emerged precisely in the most sexually-liberated countries in the world --England, Scandinavia, and the United States. The anti-war movement reached its apotheosis of rage against the government long after that same government had begun to pull out of Vietnam. Our cities live in fear of atomic bombs falling on them, but life in the cities of America today is for millions very much as it might be *after* an atomic bomb has fallen.

Peter F. Drucker in *Managing for Results* has shown how in any human organization or situation ninety percent of the events are caused by ten percent. Most human attention is allocated to the ninety percent area which is the area of problems. The ten percent area is the area of irritation and also of opportunity.

An after-the-fact articulation of what you have done usually follows upon the doing. But because we have causes and effects backwards, we mistake the articulation of what has been done as a call to do, or as a prediction about what will be done.

The youth revolution considers itself causal of things to come. It is: but of unpredictable things to come!

In reality the youth revolution is an effect of the electronic revolution. It causes things it cannot predict. In so doing

226

the youth revolution renders Marxist determination absolutely antiquated. Marxist theory insists that the future is predictable in the light of Marxist science. Dubious even when
applied to the mechanical age, Marxist determinism is simply
dead in the age of the indeterminism of Heisenberg
and the multi-level interfacing of electronic technology.
The one thing Marxism can never handle is the *now.*

To marshall effects as Revel and others have done, and then
deduce a coming revolution is to confuse effects with causes
and to render both linear and unilateral. The revolutionary
consequences of electronic technology --discontinuity and
simultaneity of information, total exposure to data from
everywhere in the world-- have had multi-level effects.
They decentralize society as they simultaneously decentralize the centers of power within society. Both governed
and governors fall under this disintegrating action.

A hypothetical proposition is demanded here, not because
it is illustrative but because it is demonstrative. *If* electronic
power --with all the enormous consequences such power
involves-- were a one-way street occupied by the national
state or a competing majority belonging to the national
state which seized power; *if* --continuing the fairy tale--
this electronic takeover were effected within a society
substantially unaffected by the electronic but also created
by the mechanical technology's genius for uniformizing a
community, then it would follow that the hardware for
a new and frightening totalitarianism would fall upon the
body politic. The historical moment when this could
have happened has already passed because of multi-
level global media interraction.

The European slow-down of electronic and televised politics
makes that continent an admirable field for government
by television *at* the moment *for* a moment.

The hypothetical is rendered actual by the historical moment
within which the United States and, to a lesser extent,

227

Canada, lives, An electronically-structured government, be it legitimate or Praetorian, bends the entire weight of the new technology to the governed. It finds, it must find, that the governed are no longer governed in accordance to modes structured into existence four centuries ago, thanks to spatialized centralization and print-dominated homogeneity.

Telepolitical dynamism has already created a swarm of Neurons --of totally involved kinship groups-- that cannot be governed telepolitically.

3 Can Telepolitics be Killed

Telepolitics has already destroyed the basis demanded for the centralized use of electronics by public power. The lesson here for moralists bent on saving the national state is obvious: kill Telepolitics! The lesson for Machiavellians bent on power is equally obvious: Telepolitics works best where television has not already altered the social fabric; where society is still relatively homogeneous; where the new clans have not corroded nationalist loyalty.

The Machiavellian solution is no longer possible for the American continent north of the Rio Grande. Possession of electronic hardware gives momentary, and probably despotic, power to those having it. They can exercise this power, however, only as one tribal organization against others. The technological basis for the old-fashioned state is today dead. The theoretical objections to that kind of state were hammered out in print by both Catholic European traditionalists and atheist anarchists during the past centuries. But neither traditionalism nor anarchism has destroyed the state. It was not killed by the friends of the Middle Ages, nor by the friends of Proudhon.

Technology has killed the state, and while presidential candidates may call America home, the haunting cry of Thomas Wolfe is in our ears: "You can't go home again! "

For "home" is no longer where it was. In the electronic age, "home" is everywhere, anywhere, and nowhere.

4 The Obsolescence of "Isms"

Conventional political labeling tended to group western parties into "nationalists" as opposed to "socialists." In those days, not all that long ago, a "nationalist" was considered to be a man opposed to socialism. Socialism, so went the current mythology, stood for the rights of labor against capital; for an international brotherhood of working men against the narrow interests of local capitalism.

Nationalism, in turn, designated the fellow willing to fight for the nation within which he was born and raised, regardless of economic consequences. Yesterday, the "nationalist" label was often identified with the "socialist" in total opposition to the international pretensions of the historic socialist movement. Fascism, of course, was a romantic effort to blend both socialism and nationalism against reaction on the Right and Bolshevism on the Left.

The temptation of socialist movements towards nationalism and the guilt complex socialists suffered earlier in the century were revealed in World War I. The Internationalist Socialist Movement expected the workers everywhere in Western Europe to prevent the war. Nonetheless, when the soldiers began to march --everywhere-- both French Socialists and German Socialists rallied to their nationalist governments.

The socialists in Germany voted supplies for the war in 1914 and gave to Kaiser Wilhelm II his finest moment. Descending from the throne and mingling in the Reichstadt with representatives of all parties, he declared: *"Ich kenne kein mehr Partein; ich kenne nur Deutschen.* --I no longer recognize parties; I recognize only Germans." That was the slogan: neither socialist worker nor Prussian landholder; only Germans, all together, in the trenches.

But World War II revealed a profound and sinister change. In Germany the national state stood, but the state itself was based on a tribal concept of blood and soil, not citizenship in the older Roman and Greek understanding of the term.

Russia, representing an international messianic movement but itself a national state in structure, returned to the mystique of the holy soil in 1941 and 1942 when Nazism knocked at the doors of Moscow.

The right of dissent, in turn, was totally denied in both the United States and Canada. Any GI sneezing in German in his sleep was likely to be turned in to the FBI and investigated. Thousands of American and Canadian citizens of Japanese descent were uprooted from their homes and sent to concentration camps. It was not treason but the mere possibility of treason that was punished.

Today it is gravely doubtful that at this moment of our history a President could get a nationally-conscripted army to fight outside the continental limits of the United States.

We pass no moral judgments; we indicate a profound sea change in the spirit of man. The kind of homogeneity possible earlier in the century is gone. It was ended by a new technology.

5 Treason as Honor

Veterans stream home from Asia through San Francisco, peace signs on their fingertips. An anti-war salute in 1944 would have been treason. But men have changed.
Today there is no treason because the national state no longer believes in itself. The media debate whether it is a fifth or a third of these returning soldiers who are drug addicts. This pained concern indicates that everybody in power looks upon these lads, eased gently into the body politic a few thousand at a time, as embarrassments and possible public charges.

230

Where are the diadems and the triumphal arches?

Some of the boys join the Peace Movement and make noises over television. The vast majority slip, gratefully and cynically, back into lives interrupted by the Vietnam interlude. A minority, in bitterness, nurse their resentment against a society that would not let them win.

As soldiers these men were seen more glaringly by the entire nation over television than any other army any time in the history of the world. But as returning soldiers they are the very least-seen veterans in history.

There are no heroes anymore. Calley and Medina have become symbols but their symbolism is so ambiguous that it can work both ways: and both officers worked Left and Right side of the road. The Left sympathized with them because they were victims of the military-industrial complex that used them. The Right sympathized with them because they were betrayed by the military-industrial complex that sent them out to do its bidding and then did not protect them.

Moralists proclaimed the Calley trial as a "great leap" forward in the corporate human conscience. For the first time in history, a major nation tried publicly one of its officers for war crimes while that war was still in progress. An underlying war between the communication systems of the media and the military reluctantly forced the army to put itself on global trial. The outcome of these trials far transcended what happened to Calley or Medina.

Diadems and triumphal arches are for returning heroes who saved their nation. There are no diadems and triumphal arches because there is no longer any nation.

6 The Presidential Dilemma and the Work Ethic

The President is the most powerful man in the free world.
He is even more powerful, probably, than any counterpart
within the Communist world.

Yet how can this man govern a nation, a third or fourth
part of which has abdicated from the national state?

How can this man handle a citizenry the bare majority of
which thinks of itself as belonging principally to the state
with all its American orthodoxy?

Where is the consensus without which the President, Congress
and the Judiciary cannot function?

What, any more, constitutes the American way of life?
What is its faith?

What can such a man do when the orthodoxy he represents
is constituted by a generic set of principles that cannot be
converted into televised images?

He can, and does, appeal to older cultural symbols now
floating much like the weightless particles in the astronauts'
space vehicle through the crumbling social fabric of the
American psyche. The oldest of these as outlined in the
documents of the founding fathers and expressed through a
dominantly puritan culture for two hundred years is the
"work ethic."

America was uniquely the land of opportunity, where any
man could *work,* and if he worked hard enough, no matter
what his background, he could then "get ahead."

The temporary cooling off from 1968 to 1970 with its
subsequent decline in mass demonstrations, the burning of
cities and disruption of universities, was accompanied by the
suggestion cried for in high places, that America return to

the old work ethic. All will be well if the nation can only come again to love work, as did its forefathers. President Nixon, Secretary of the Treasury Connally, Secretary of Commerce Maurice Stans, reiterated this conviction. Mr. Stans on *Meet the Press,* January 30, 1972, insisted that the question did not have to do with the quantity of work done but with the quality. Secretary Connally, in the face of the dollar crisis, urged both labor and management groups to get the nation working again.

Senator McGovern in his speech accepting the presidential nomination of the Democratic Party also echoed the call to Americans to return to work.

The telepolitical question is, "Working at *what?* "

How can you get a *rich* nation working again when the "poverty of affluence" has seeped into the bloodstream of its young? What is so special about work for a youth whose technological base has conditioned it for leisure?

The resurrection of the work ethic is an effort to bring back a dead national attitude after its technological base has been destroyed. The work ethic marches through American mythology as an empty symbol.

7 Blood, Womb, Clan

The democratic creed was fashioned out of a series of propositions linked in a linear fashion that produced a number of conclusions about the nature of man and politics. Reflecting the Cartesian confidence in pure reason that dominated the Enlightenment, shaping before the visual imagination a free man with natural rights who was linked to neither blood nor soil, the old democratic creed was principally an argument and a conclusion whose parts were linked together by connections as mechanically visual as are the parts of an automobile.

233

Just as a manual on general mechanics can be applied to any
and all automobiles that enter a shop, the democratic faith
depended on univocally repeatable units such as universal
conscription, universal laws, and universal franchise. Applicable everywhere in precisely the same way, the old world
had as its ground a Newtonian space in which objects and
men can be fitted and linked together by linear "connections."
That world has now disappeared in an acoustic space in
which everything is center and nothing is periphery, everything is unique and nothing is connected by geometric
linearity.

Electronic technology creates multiple centers, without mar-
gins --and does it in an instant and omnipresent way. There
were no longer any ex-plosions into a fixed space waiting to
be filled up by democratic men and states.

The now im-plosion is not centrifugal. Even though the
legions of jet aircraft scatter men rapidly around the globe,
each man remains uniquely a center wherever he is. Daniel
Boorstin * has written shrewdly on the lost art of travel.
"The traveler used to go about the world to encounter the
natives. A function of travel agencies now is to prevent this
encounter. They are always devising efficient new ways
of insulating the tourist from the travel world."

With old-fashioned space and time domesticated, shriveled
into insignificance in the new electronic world of total simultaneity and a new ubiquity of all to all, the old ground has
disappeared. The electronic tribe returned because it was
the *only* spatio-temporal integration left a mankind that
found itself floating everywhere at once like astronauts in
space for whom "up" and "down" have ceased to be categories of the real. The personal returned as figure because
its older ground in space-time was destroyed.

The Image: A Guide to Pseudo Events in America (New York:
Harper & Row, 1961)

234

8 The Show Must Go On

Television shapes personal images, not abstract principles such as democracy. Its tactile sensuousness beckons men to return to the blood, the womb, the clan --but to a blood, womb, and clan fixed in no ground but everywhere at once.

The image of the astronaut is extremely helpful in this situation. Whatever astronauts *do* in space is done by the moving of information which is central to electronic technology. The distinction between the man who does something and the man who reports on the event is irrelevant. Computers bring down lunar modules and the huge teams of scientists and technicians are literally --in terms of the electronic wraparound, electronic existence-- as much on the surface of the moon as are the astronauts themselves. Who brings down a 747 in pea-soup weather? The team running the computers below or the pilot? Certainly we must answer that both bring the 747 down, but both do so by exchanging information. Hardware is at the service of software everywhere.

The newspaper age began with journals like Addison and Steele's *The Spectator*. The assumption underlying these precursors of the newspaper was Newtonian: i.e. there is a world of things and men going on "out there" and we "here" --in our print shop-- are reporting on what is happening there. From this assumption, often violated in practice because nobody can doubt that the Addisons and Steeles really wanted to change things in England through the exercise of gentle ironic moralizing, there grew into history and hardened into myth the conviction that men who move information must only "report," that they cannot "do." The obverse of the coin insisted that men who do --the politicians-- must keep their hands off communication systems. These last are the province of the so-called "free press." Everybody is free to communicate except the government, about which everybody else reports.

These hidden biases, as suggested, were behind the controversy between the American defense structure and CBS.
Ironically enough, two communication systems failed to
communicate. This failure rendered impossible any sensible
discussion to say nothing about any sensible disagreement.
The issue was complicated in that by an anachronistic irony
both the Defense Department and the Pentagon had to defend themselves against television media on those same
hostile stations.

The time is fast approaching when the Pentagon and the
government will defend and counterattack on their own
stations. The deep and underlying anxiety which gripped
the three major networks when the Vice President and
others rose to the defense of the Pentagon is rooted in an
incipient awareness that there is no ontological reason why
everybody, including the government, cannot put on its
own show.

9 Drop-Out, Drop-In

There are tensions within that could very well be the seeds
of further decomposition. This decomposition could be a
further decentralization of the old doctrinal or racial tribe
into an even smaller familial clan. The technological hardware is now in existence enabling man, should he so desire,
to retire more intimately into an even warmer womb, that
of the atomic family.

We speak of the atomic family rather than the extended
family which englobes grandparents, aunts, uncles, cousins,
etc. because the atomic family has historically dominated
the most industrialized regions of the United States. Given
the possibility of working at home (whatever "work" and
"home" are) while tuned in, not to a center of work, but
to one's role, it is not at all impossible that millions of men
and women will simply stay in their houses and, in Voltaire's
terms, "tend their own garden."

This conclusion must be qualified delicately. A massive return to the family in Anglo-American society is possible *only* if the desire for privacy continues to wither away. Traditionally, the American male flees the family in order to find privacy. Privacy is "outside space" and the public life is "enclosed space." Latin males find privacy at home and live publicly in the forum, in the streets, in cafes, bars and restaurants. Dropping-out of the family is dropping-into privacy in the United States. Dropping-into the family and out of the street is privacy for the Hispanic world. If the continued decay of privacy in Anglo-American youth carries over into maturity and middle age, a Latin family structure might very well replace the traditional American one. The new communes suggest this possibility.

In order to live comfortably within the cohesive depth pattern of totally involved kinship groups, men must have forgotten the very meaning of privacy, that inheritance of the later modern world. But forgetfulness takes time. It may even take a generation or two. Electronic speed-up has moved everyone over thirty from mechanical linearity --collective homogeneity--interposed by moments of treasured privacy, into the vortex of neuronic participation. The abrasiveness and the heat of cultural clan structures have been produced by the apparently "cool" medium of television. There is an undercurrent today of withdrawal from the tribe by men who have spent a decade or so involved in fierce tribal loyalties. Where are the flower children? Will electronic clans be as ephemeral as is a flower, blooming and fading with the passing seasons?

The flight from the home would not be back to the older public orthodoxy of the citizen. It would be the fiercest of all individualisms, more rugged than that individualism which was extolled as part of the popular piety of the United States. But neither a return to the family nor the flight of the individual could turn *off* the media. Both individual and familial clan would be as beamed on as is the largest of tribes.

237

It is possible that tribal, familial and individualistic structures will co-exist in a kind of interfacing in which each facet mirrors the others. The frozen structure as a model belongs to antiquity. Instead of dropping *out* of one or another cultural pattern, men will be constantly dropping *in* to them without leaving the others behind. Backwards and forwards are terms with no meaning.

Now, as Eastern and Western cultures cross-fertilize one another, Western Man must face squarely the problem of continuity, while Eastern Man cannot escape the problem of technology as related to his ancestral and cherished ways of life.

Drop-out means not only drop-out from the system. It can and does mean drop-out from the tribe and from the family. But what one cannot do is drop out of the technology. What is the new technology that will be NEW to the electronic?

Radical discontinuity pushed to its existential limit is the lonely individual, the shipwrecked Robinson Crusoe, but a Robinson Crusoe who has chosen to be shipwrecked. Electronic rim-spin which unites every man with every man does so by decentralizing. The ultimate consequences of this decentralization would undo the technology itself.

The perfection of any technology is its failure, as Juenger insists. The perfection of Newtonian space is its contrary, acoustic space.

Neuronic families and decentralization are no more eternal than were nationalism and centralization. But whatever the future might bring, neuronization is the springboard to that future if not that very future itself.

Bibliography

Anderson, Jack and Kalvelage, Carl. *American Government --Like It Is.* General Learning Press, Morristown, N.J. 1972.

Boguslaw, Robert. *The New Utopians.* Prentice-Hall, Englewood Cliffs, N.J. 1965.

Boorstin, Daniel J. *The Genius of American Politics.* University of Chicago Press, 1953.
----- *The Image.* Harper & Row, New York, 1964.

Carrel, Alexis, *Man The Unknown.* Harper & Row, 1939.

Casty, Alan. *Mass Media and Mass Man.* Holt, Rinehart and Winston, New York, 1968.

Cherry, Colin. *On Human Communication.* The M.I.T. Press, Cambridge, Mass., 1966.

Cirlot, J.E. *A Dictionary of Symbols.* tr. by Jack Sage. Philosophical Library, New York, 1962.

Cropsey, Joseph. *Ancients and Moderns, essays on the tradition of political philosophy in honor of Leo Strauss.* Basic Books, New York, 1964.

Curti, Merle. *American Paradox, The Conflict of Thought and Action.* Rutgers University Press, New Brunswick, N.J., 1956.

Descartes, René. *Discourse on Method.* tr. by John Veitch. Open Court Publishing, LaSalle, Ill., 1946.

Diamond, Martin. *The Democratic Republic.* Rand McNally, Chicago, 1966.

D'Ors, Alvaro. *Forma de Gobierno y Legitimidad Familiar,* O Crece O Muere, Madrid, 1960.

Donosco Cortés, Juan. *Obras Completas.* ed. introducción y notas de Carlos Valverde. Biblioteca de Autores Cristianos, Madrid, 1970.

Drucker, Peter F. *Technology, Management and Society.* Harper & Row, New York, 1970.

Eliade, Mircea. *Myth and Reality.* Harper & Row, New York, 1963.

Fortescue, Sir John. *De Laudibus LegumAnglie.* ed. and tr. by S.B. Chrimes, Cambridge University Press, 1949.

Frye, Northrop. *The Modern Century.* Oxford University Press, New York, 1967.

Fuller, R. Buckminster. *I Seem to be a Verb.* Bantam Books, New York, 1970.
-----*Untitled Epic Poem on the History of Industrialization.* Simon & Schuster, New York, 1962.
-----*Utopia or Oblivion: The Prospects for Humanity.* Bantam Books, New York, 1969.

Giedion, Siegfried. *Mechanization Takes Command.* Oxford University Press, New York, 1970.
-----*Space, Time and Architecture.* Harvard University Press, Cambridge, Mass. 1967.

Gilson, Etienne. *Réalisme Thomiste et Critique de la Connaissance.* Librairie Philosophique J. Vrin, Paris, 1947.

Groulx, Lionel. *Histoire du Canada français depuis la découverte, 2 vols.* Fides, Montreal, 1969..

Guardini, Romano. *Power and Responsibility.* tr. by Elmor C. Briefs. Henry Regnery, Chicago, 1961.

Habsburg, Otto von. *Charles V.* tr. by Michael Ross. Praeger, New York, 1970.

Hall, Edward T. *The Silent Language.* Doubleday, Garden City, N.Y., 1959.

Hamilton, Alexander; Jay, John; Madison, James. *The Federalist Papers.* intro. by Clinton Rossiter. New American Library, New York, 1961.

Hayakawa, S.I. *Language in Thought and Action.* Harcourt Brace and World, New York, 1963.

Hobbes, Thomas. *Leviathan.* ed. W.G.P. Smith. Oxford at the Clarendon Press, 1943.

Hoffer, Eric. *The Ordeal of Change.* Harper & Row, New York, 1963.

Hulzinga, Johann. *Homo Ludens, A Study of the Play Element in Culture.* Beacon Press, Boston, 1955.

Illich, Ivan. *De-Schooling Society.* Harper & Row, New York, 1971.

Innis, Harold A. *The Bias of Communication.* University of Toronto Press, 1964.

Jackson, Don D., Ed. *Communication, Family, and Marriage: Human Communication, Vol. I.* Science and Behavior Books, Palo Alto, Calif., 1970.

Johnson, Lyndon Baines. *The Vantage Point, Perspectives of the Presidency, 1963-1969.* Holt, Rinehart and Winston, New York,1971.

Juenger, Friedrich Georg. *The Failure of Technology.* Henry Regnery, Chicago, 1949.
----- *Die Spiele, Ein Schlüssel zu Ihren Bedeutung.* Klosterman, Franfurt, 1953.

Jung, Carl. *Man and His Symbols.* Dell, New York, 1968.

Juvenal, Bertrand de. *On Power.* tr. by J.F. Huntington, Beacon Press, Boston, 1962.

Kant, Immanuel. *Critique of Pure Reason.* tr. by F. Max Müller, 2nd ed. rev., Macmillan, New York, 1927.

Kinser, Bill and Kleinman, Neil. *The Dream that Was no More than a Dream.* Harper & Row, New York, 1969.

Kendall, Willmoore. *The Conservative Affirmation.* Henry Regnery, Chicago, 1963.
-----*Willmoore Kendall Contra Mundum.* ed. by Nellie D. Kendall. Arlington House, New Rochelle, N.Y., 1971.
----- and Carey, George W. *The Basic Symbols of the American Political Tradition.* Louisiana University Press, Baton Rouge, 1970.

Koestler, Arthur. *The Act of Creation.* Dell, New York, 1967.

Kracauer, Siegfried. *Theory of Film.* Oxford, New York, 1970.

McDayter, Walt. Ed., *A Media Mosaic: Canadian Communications Through a Critical Eye.* Holt, Rinehart and Winston of Canada, Montreal, 1971.

McGinniss, Joe. *The Selling of the President.* Pocket Book edition, Simon & Schuster, 1970.

McLuhan, Marshall and Watson, Wilfred. *From Cliche to Archetype.* The Viking Press, New York, 1970.
----- and Nevitt, Berrington. *Take Today: The Executive as Drop Out.* Longmans Canada, Toronto 1972.
-----*The Gutenberg Galaxy.* University of Toronto Press, 1966.
----- and Parker, Harley. *Through the Vanishing Point: Space in Poetry and Painting.* Harper & Row, New York, 1968.
-----*Understanding Media: The Extensions of Man.* McGraw Hill, New York, 1964.
-----and Quentin, Fiore. *War and Peace in the Global Village.* Bantam Books, New York, 1968.

McNamara, Eugene. *The Interior Landscape: The Literary Criticism of Marshall McLuhan 1943-1962.* McGraw Hill, New York, 1969.

Marcel, Gabriel. *Les Hommes Contre L'Humain.* Ed. du Vieux Columbier, Paris, 1951.

Marcuse, Herbert. *One Dimensional Man.* Beacon Press, Boston, 1968.

Mumford, Lewis. *Technics and Civilization.* Harcourt, Brace and World, New York, 1963.
----- *The Highway and the City.* Harcourt, Brace and World, New York, 1963.

Ong, Walter J. *The Barbarian Within.* Macmillan, New York, 1962.

Ortega y Gasset, José. *Obras.* Espasa Calpe, S.A. Madrid, 1932.

Parker, Francis. "A Realistic Epistomology" in *The Return to Reason*. ed. by John Wild, Henry Regnery, Chicago, 1953.

Percy, Walker. *Love in the Ruins*. Dell, New York, 1972.

Picard, Max. *Man and Language*. Henry Regnery, Chicago, 1963.

Rabade, Romeo and Trespalacios, Fernandez. *Historia del Pensamiento Filosófico y Cientifico,* sexta ed., Gregorio des Toro, Madrid, 1969.

Rahner, Hugo. *Der Spielende Mensch*. Johannes Verlag, Einsiedeln, 1948.

Richards, I.A. *Design for Escape*. Harcourt, Brace and World, New York, 1968.

Ruesch, Jungen, M.D., *Therapeutic Communication*. W.W. Norton, New York, 1961.

Simon, Herbert A., *The Shape of Automation for Men and Management*. Harper & Row, New York, 1965.

Simon, Yves. *The Philosophy of Democratic Government*. University of Chicago Press, 1951.

Sloan, Thomas. *Quebec, The Not So Quiet Revolution*. Ryerson Press, Toronto, 1965.

Stewart, Walter. *Shrug: Trudeau in Power*. New Press, Toronto, 1971.

Strauss, Leo. *The Political Philosophy of Hobbes*. University of Chicago Press, 1959.

Toffler, Alvin. *Future Shock*. Bantam Books, New York. 1971.

Thomas Aquinas, *Le "De Ente et Essentia" texte établi d'aprés les manuscrits parisiens, intro. notes et études historiques par M.-D. Roland-Gosselin, O.P.* Librairie Philosophique J. Vrin, Paris, 1948.

Voeglin, Eric. *The New Science of Politics.* University of Chicago Press, 1952.

Wiener, Norbert. *Cybernetics or Control and Communication in the Animal and the Machine.* The M.I.T. Press, Cambridge, Mass. 1961.

Wilhelmsen, Frederick D. *Man's Knowledge of Reality.* Prentice-Hall, Englewood Cliffs, N.J. 1946.
-----and Bret, Jane. *The War in Man: Media and Machines.* University of Georgia Press, Athens, Ga. 1970.

Williams, Raymond. *Communications.* Penguin Books, London, 1966.

Wills, Garry. *The Second Civil War, Arming for Armageddon.* Signet Book, New American Library, New York, 1968.

Youngblood, Gene. *Expanded Cinema.* E.P. Dutton, New York, 1970.

Index

247

Rockefeller Family 134
Rogers, William 211, 212
Rolling Stone Newspaper 197
Rome / Roman Empire 24, 40, 41,
52, 66, 73, 95, 111, 134, 146, 182,
189, 200, 216, 230
Roosevelt, Franklin 117, 108, 143
Roosevelt Era 153
Rousseau, Jean-Jacques 155, 161,
167
Ruby, Jack 21, 93
Russia /Russian -- see USSR

Saint Patrick's Day 102
Saint-Jean Baptiste Day /Society 86,
88, 128
Salan, General 53
Salant, Richard 107, 109
Salazar 133
Salisbury 220
San Francisco 28, 217, 230
San Francisco State College 179
Satan / Satanism 21, 128
Scandinavia / Scandiavians 138, 142,
226
Schafley, Phyllis 197
Schlesinger, Arthur 131
Scotland and the Scots 73, 200
Scott, Sir Walter 35
Senaca 79
Sept-Iles, Quebec 91
Sevareid, Eric 16, 56, 87, 96, 117
Seville, Spain 84
Shakespeare and his times 29
Sharp, Mitchell 212
Sherbrooke, Quebec 91
Sicily/ Sicilian 148
Simon, Yves 151, 163
Sirhan, Sirhan 21, 93
Skinner, B.F. 186
Smith, Rev. Gerald K. 117
Smith, Howard K. 16, 56, 87, 100
Smoot, Dan 197
Sobickel, Richard 23
Socrates 59
Sorensen, Theodore 131
South Africa 97-99
South America 65, 90, 126, 167,
170, 171, 217
Soviet Union --See USSR

Spain 59, 71, 77-81, 85, 90, 126,
168, 194
Spanish Armada 195
Spanish Civil War 77-81
Spectator, The 235
Spivak, Lawrence 120
Stalin, Joseph 133, 143
Stanfield, Robert 187
Stans, Maurice 233
Steele, Richard 235
Stormer, John 197
Streisand, Barbra 149
Students for a Democratic Society
(SDS) 174, 196, 198
Sudan, The 59
Supreme Court (U.S.) 32, 169, 171

Tacitus 24
Taiwan 199
Tannenberg 209
Tate, Sharon 21
Teilhard de Chardin, Pierre 38
Tennessee 153
Texas 136
Thackeray, William Makepeace 35
Thibon, Gustave 43
Third Reich 186
Thomas Aquinas, Saint 181
Today Show 117, 170, 213
Tokyo 49
"Tokyo Rose" 113
Tremblay, Michel 90
Trotsky, Leon 133
Trudeau, Pierre Elliott 28, 84, 122,
127, 128, 130, 149, 187, 188, 211,
214
Truman, Harry 192, 193
Turkey / Turkish 205
TVA (Tennessee Valley Authority)
153

Uganda 64
Ukraine, The 196
Ulster 101, 102, 104
Unamuno, Miguel de 78
Union (in Civil War) 162, 184
United Jewish Defense League (JDL)
23
United Nations, The 77, 198, 199,
217

Printed and bound by
The Kingsport Press, Inc., Kingsport, Tenn.